THE HIDDENNESS ARGUMENT

'A powerful and yet simple statement of one of the most powerful and yet simple arguments for atheism that has been developed in recent years.'

T. J. Mawson, Edgar Jones Fellow in Philosophy, St Peter's College, Oxford University, author of *Belief in God*

'Had I read John Schellenberg's brilliant new work, which gives title and cogency to the argument from the hiddenness of God, I would have become an unbeliever years before. In fact, of all the arguments for and against God's existence (and I've heard them all) this is the most powerful I have encountered in support of the atheist position. A tour de force.'

Michael Shermer, Publisher *Skeptic* magazine, monthly columnist *Scientific American*, author of *The Moral Arc*

'One of the things that has struck me the most about the development of Schellenberg's thought is precisely his optimism about human reason and its prospects. The spirit of Schellenberg's work is never one of pessimistic judgment about the errors and superstitions of religious folk. He is not a mocker. Rather, his writing seems to flow from a conviction that there's so much out there to explore.'

Adam Green, *Notre Dame Philosophical Reviews*

'Freshmen philosophy students could understand and benefit from this book. It is ideal for introductions to philosophy or undergraduate courses in the philosophy of religion.'

Chris Tucker, *Faith and Philosophy*

'If his classroom is anything like his book, Schellenberg must be a great teacher . . . Schellenberg has masterfully articulated an elegant argument . . . This book deserves careful study and it belongs on the shelf of every person interested in questions of theology and philosophy of religion.'

Randal Rauser, *The Tentative Apologist blog*

J. L. SCHELLENBERG

THE HIDDENNESS ARGUMENT

Philosophy's New Challenge to Belief in God

OXFORD
UNIVERSITY PRESS

Great Clarendon Street, Oxford, OX2 6DP,
United Kingdom

Oxford University Press is a department of the University of Oxford.
It furthers the University's objective of excellence in research, scholarship,
and education by publishing worldwide. Oxford is a registered trade mark of
Oxford University Press in the UK and in certain other countries

First published 2015
First published in paperback 2017

Published in the United States of America by Oxford University Press
198 Madison Avenue, New York, NY 10016, United States of America

British Library Cataloguing in Publication Data
Data available

Library of Congress Cataloging in Publication Data
Data available

ISBN 978–0–19–873308–9 (Hbk.)
ISBN 978–0–19–880117–7 (Pbk.)

For Regina

PREFACE TO THE PAPERBACK EDITION

A reviewer of this book suggests that its first three chapters might profitably be read in reverse order: 3, 2, 1 instead of 1, 2, 3. I think this is an excellent idea and recommend it to my readers.

PREFACE

In the past twenty years or so a new argument against the existence of God has emerged in philosophy. Some call it the argument from divine hiddenness. I prefer a leaner, less misleading label: *the hiddenness argument*. Its basic thought is that the existence of God invites our belief less strongly than it would in a world created by God. In many places and times, and for many people, God's existence has been rather less than a clear fact, and according to the hiddenness argument, this is a reason to suppose that it is not a fact at all.

When reasoning is given a name in this way—*the* hiddenness argument—it sounds as though exactly one strand of argumentation is being referred to. So it should be noted that what we have here is really a *way* of reasoning, of which there can be many instances. This is certainly what you find when you examine older reasoning about God, such as the cosmological argument, which uses the idea of God to explain why there is a cosmos, or its sister the teleological or design argument, which uses the same idea to explain the order that prevails in the cosmos. By now there are many different versions of both the cosmological argument and the teleological argument. In the case of the hiddenness argument, some variety has already emerged; no doubt there is more to come. But I'll be concerned primarily with the instance of reasoning that started the contemporary discussion and remains at the center of the hiddenness debate among philosophers as the twenty-first century inches toward its third decade. This happens to be an argument I created, and both I and others have for some time now been calling it the hiddenness argument. I'll be continuing the practice here.

There are hints in the history of philosophy as to the possibility of an atheistic argument of this kind, and to that extent the suggestion that what we have is a brand new way of reasoning should come with a qualification. But no actual *reasoning*—no developed atheistic argument along these lines—appeared until I put together such an argument in my first book, *Divine Hiddenness and Human Reason*, which was published in the spring of 1993. In that book I tried to get clear about *how* and *why* we wouldn't expect God to be hidden from us, and assessed a wide array of possible replies to the resulting argument.

Because of discussion this book aroused, the hiddenness argument is now quite regularly explored alongside the venerable old problem of evil in philosophy classrooms and texts. (The problem of evil is an argument or set of arguments against God based on facts about the *bad* things that happen in the world. As we'll see, the hiddenness argument's approach is not to suggest that hiddenness is bad.) Articles on the hiddenness argument have now appeared many times over not only in philosophy journals and books but also in the various Companions and Handbooks on the philosophy of religion put out by presses such as Oxford, Cambridge, Routledge, and Wiley-Blackwell, and in the Macmillan, Routledge, and Stanford encyclopedias of philosophy. The argument (though sometimes in a form that seems to me pitiably malnourished) is moreover frequently seen in discussions of the existence of God online. It looks to be here to stay.

Naturally, I'm pleased that this bit of reasoning from my early days in philosophy has received so much attention. But at the same time I'm inclined to emphasize how simple an argument it is! And I am fascinated by the social and cultural facts that prevented it from being developed much sooner (versions of which still cause it to be overlooked or misstated both by theists, those who believe in God, and by atheists, who deny that God exists). As I've often said, it confirms our evolutionary immaturity that such relatively uncomplicated arguments still need to be discovered. One wonders how many other philosophical arguments will be dug up in centuries to come.

A good deal of the attention that the hiddenness argument has received, as is customary in philosophy, is highly critical. Some of the material that has been published, especially recently, has struck me as quite impressive. Some seems to me to leave much to be desired. It's tempting to speculate on the reasons for the combination of interest and anxiety, sometimes joined to subtle tendencies of misstatement, that the hiddenness argument apparently provokes among many believers in God. But I will resist that temptation here.

What I *do* want to do is to provide an accessible, brief, but vigorous statement of the hiddenness argument and an explanation of the associated issues designed for wide consumption that clearly distinguishes the hiddenness argument from the problem of evil and establishes its claim to attention in discussions of theism and atheism. After three opening chapters, what you will find is careful reasoning that seeks to make crystal clear just what the hiddenness argument is and why it matters. Some readers may want more details or wish to see more attention to the broad academic literature on related subjects. To them I commend my own academic work on hiddenness issues in philosophy, which provides many more details and is far more thorough in certain respects, and of course also the long string of related works by others. Both can be found listed in the bibliography at the back of the book.

What I've said so far might suggest that what you hold in your hands is some sort of academic "Introduction" to hiddenness reasoning. I want to emphasize that this is not the case. Though, given my attention to fundamentals, aim of clarity, and many explanations, the style of this book at times overlaps with that of a straightforward "introduction to x," I have also felt free to depart from such a style at various points. I would like to interest people in philosophical work who might have wondered what it's all about, and also to provide a different example of traditional atheism than can be found in the "new" atheists. For this reason tufts of my experience as a believer and as a nonbeliever will not be out of place. Readers can expect to find them here and there in the book. In a culture in which people are regularly herded into one of two camps, theists (those who believe in God) and naturalists (those who think nature is all there is), it may be useful to have an example of how atheism can arise without naturalism, and even in someone broadly sympathetic to religion. Indeed, this is one aspect of the hiddenness phenomenon.

I should offer a word about the relation between this book and my previous book on *Evolutionary Religion*, which was also designed for a wide readership. In a way I'm circling back here and re-engaging a discussion that occupied me long before I had ever thought of such a thing as evolutionary religion. Some may wonder why I would do so instead of marching on linearly. Well, there is the reason already mentioned: the need for a clear and crisp statement of an argument still rightly called new, for whose well-being (or at least proper apprehension) I feel somewhat responsible. But it wouldn't be wrong to think of this book as also being a kind of "prequel" to the other. When proposing, in the other, a skeptical-imaginative form of religion compatible with atheism that, to my mind, is well adapted to our place in evolutionary time, I was, obviously, moving in a rather lightly populated domain. Why should I expect anyone to pay attention to my pioneering efforts in that domain when the idea of theism, the notion that there is a person-like God, still tugs so strongly?

I hope this book will help to lessen that tugging, and open us to the thought that other even more interesting religious ideas may await us in evolution's future.

ACKNOWLEDGMENTS

I've been thinking about the topics of this book, off and on, for nearly thirty years. Over that time I have discussed its topics in many settings, and been helped by many people. Colleagues, students, audience members, internet provocateurs—I thank you all.

But certain people deserve special thanks. My teachers in philosophy of religion, Terence Penelhum and Richard Swinburne, for example, who gave much friendly support to my first attempts to articulate the hiddenness problem. And for generous encouragement and support (almost) ever since, including much incisive criticism, I am greatly indebted to Paul Draper and Dan Howard-Snyder. Dan has been particularly active in the hiddenness discussion; its flourishing owes an enormous amount to his efforts. Others who have provided generous help include Bill Alston, Steve Maitzen, Jason Marsh, Wes Morriston, Alexander Pruss, John Thorp, and Bill Wainwright.

Two recent events reawakened my interest in the hiddenness discusion after I had been preoccupied with other themes for more than a decade. One was a two-day focus on that subject during a philosophy of religion summer seminar at the University of St. Thomas in Saint Paul, Minnesota in June of 2011, and the other was a conference on the epistemology of atheism held at the Université de Lorraine in Nancy, France in June 2013. I am grateful to the organizers and all the sharp participants, and particularly want to thank Peter van Inwagen and Dean Zimmerman in the former case, and Roger Pouivet and John Greco in the latter, for stimulating conversation and for supporting my work.

As for the book itself—*this* book—I'd like to express my gratitude to everyone at Oxford University Press who worked on it, and particularly to Peter Momtchiloff. The comments of anonymous reviewers for Oxford University Press are also much appreciated. Klaas Kraay saved me much time by lending to this effort a hiddenness bibliography he had independently compiled, to which I made only a few additions and small adjustments. I am grateful.

The book owes its existence to my wife, Regina Coupar, who prodded me to write it. She also read more than one draft and gave me many helpful comments, particularly about how to make my ideas comprehensible for *everyone*. I heartily approve of this aim, and to the extent that it has been achieved, the book owes to her both its existence and its accessibility.

As for what *I* owe Regina: that could not be expressed even in many books. But this one is dedicated to her.

CONTENTS

CHAPTER 1

SOME BASIC TOOLS

Philosophers sometimes say that philosophy, unlike science, has no technical vocabulary. William James, for example, is supposed to have said that philosophy is simply "an unusually stubborn attempt to think clearly." From the everyday problems of human life you should be able to arrive at an understanding of the reasoning of philosophers just by learning to put up with a bit more precision than usual. This is what we tell our unsuspecting students. And we really believe it!

So I was surprised (read: injured, devastated) when a non-philosopher friend of mine declared himself frustrated by the "techno-babble" in my first book. Apparently I had come to take for granted a way of talking that's not immediately transparent to everyone. Of course, in that book I was mainly writing for other philosophers who I knew *would* find my language transparent. But having had this experience, and given the wider audience imagined for the present book, I'm inclined as I begin to explain a few things about philosophical reasoning that will make it easier to understand the language I use.

That concern dominates this first chapter. (If you already know how to operate philosophy's tools with basic competence, feel free to move swiftly through this material.) Though a few additional reasoning concepts are introduced and explained elsewhere in the book, my aim here is to give explanations that will provide a clear framework for understanding everything else I say about logic and related matters, suitable even for those who ordinarily find that they want to tear their hair out or throw the book away when they encounter such things. In Chapter 2 I'll also provide a conceptual map to help us accurately locate, in the vast and rugged terrain of religion, the idea of God that will be at issue in this book, and understand the terminology of "hiddenness."

Arguments

Let's start by thinking about what sort of creature an "argument" is. Though when in ordinary life we use the word "argument" we often have in mind a disagreement or fight ("Just listen to those pots and pans! Another argument!"), in philosophy the word means *reasoning*—usually a particular instance or specimen of reasoning. Not that philosophers don't ever fight and *have* arguments. But they're supposed to avoid this by *giving* arguments—careful reasoning for their point of view which respects the other person's intelligence. If you offer your opinion on some controversial matter and your conversation partner cocks her head and says "So what's your argument for that?" the word "argument" is being used in this philosophical way.

But maybe you don't want to give an argument. After all, that could take some time. Maybe you just want to express your opinion. That's fine—no one will prevent you. However if you find yourself with a gnawing need to know whether common opinions are true, you'll want a way to test them. In science, specific methods involving such things as physical experimentation have been devised to test opinions about what explains what in the natural world. But when it comes to the very general and fundamental questions which interest philosophers—for example, "Do we have free will?" "Can machines think?" "Is there a God?" "Exactly what is a natural world?"—the only test we have for opinions is to work out how we might reason in support of the opinion in question, or in opposition to it, and to think very hard about whether this reasoning is any good. (When asked what philosophy is, the famous twentieth-century philosopher Gilbert Ryle is said to have replied quite simply: "Thinking hard.") As might be expected, philosophers have therefore in the course of their subject's history turned reasoning and argumentation into something of an art.

Philosophers call the content of any opinion—what it says, whether true or false—a *proposition*. (The terms "statement" and "claim" are sometimes used synonymously with "proposition.") When you reason in support of an opinion, you are giving an argument for supposing the proposition it expresses to be true. So how do you produce such support? Well, you do it by providing other propositions that do the supporting. These supporting propositions are called *premises* and the proposition they are supposed to support is called a *conclusion*. Together, these two—premises and conclusion—constitute your argument. Every argument has at least one premise and at least one conclusion, and nothing other than premises or conclusions is to be found in arguments. When a conclusion is used as a basis for further reasoning, it gets to perform both roles. Of course these parts have to work together *properly* if the argument is to do its job, extending our knowledge of the world.

Logic

The study of what it takes for them to do so, of what makes arguments tick, is called logic. Ever since the time of Aristotle, who was the first to undertake such study systematically, philosophers have been obsessed with how to make their arguments good ones—ones that actually support a conclusion, giving us reason to believe it to be true. Because, as I've said, careful reasoning is the only way we have of coming to grips with the deep questions of philosophy, perhaps this obsession is understandable. *And no argument can be a good one without being logically correct.*

To be logically correct an argument's conclusion must "follow from" its premises, which means—at least in deductive arguments, to which category the hiddenness argument belongs—that the arguer has to use for premises propositions that have no way of being true, when taken together, unless the conclusion is true too. (Inductive arguments, which aim only at some measure of probability, must be understood differently, but they will not be playing much of a role in this book and so are ignored here.) Put the parts of the argument together in the wrong way and this won't be the case. But premises from which a conclusion does follow in the deductive sense leave you nowhere else to go; in such a case the conclusion follows *with necessity*.

Here's a simple example: from the premises *All Greeks are Europeans* and *Aristotle is a Greek*, it follows with necessity that *Aristotle is a European*. The last statement *has* to be true if the first two are. That is what it means for it to follow from them deductively or with necessity. Notice that a conclusion may follow from premises even when every proposition involved is false. (Logic is all about form, not about content.) So if I said *All fish can fly* and *Aristotle is a fish*, therefore *Aristotle can fly*, my conclusion would follow just as surely as in the first case, even though—as I hope you see!—each of these propositions is false.

Now at the end of the day, *true premises* are going to be important too. But at this point we're still just thinking about logical connections. Lots of interesting things have been discovered in logic about how propositions can be fitted together into arguments whose conclusions follow deductively from their premises. The most ingenious and illuminating ways of doing so are often thought beautiful in philosophy, just as certain experiments in science are thought beautiful.

Take, for instance, an argument derived from one of the dialogues of the ancient Greek philosopher Plato, Aristotle's teacher, which students of philosophical ethics will encounter by day two or three of an introductory course. The dialogue is named *Euthyphro*, after one of its main characters, and the argument is called the Euthyphro dilemma. The Euthyphro dilemma tests the common opinion that what is morally right can be determined only by reference to God's commands—*the Divine Command Theory of Morality* as it is often called. This dilemma argument, here religiously updated to refer to God rather than the Greek gods, begins with a premise that offers some thought-provoking options for those who accept this theory:

Either right actions are right because God commands them, or God commands them because they are right.

In other words, supposing God exists and issues commands, there are two options: either God's commands *make* the right actions right or God merely *sees* they are right and issues commands accordingly. The advocate of the Divine Command Theory must accept that it is one or the other. Then come a couple of further premises, one for each of these options. Here's the first of them:

If right actions are right because God commands them (option one), then the Divine Command Theory fails because morality is *arbitrary*, subject to God's whim and so not grounded in reasons at all.

If the first option is correct, we have something analogous to what we'd have if, when a mother tells her small child to do something "because I told you so," it really is *just because she told him so*, instead of because of some reason she's too busy to explain right now. Moreover—the other premise—

If instead God commands right actions because they are right (the second option), then the Divine Command Theory fails because morality is completely *autonomous*, grounded in reasons quite independent of God's will, reasons which we too may see if we work at it.

That is, if the second option is correct and morality is autonomous and independent of God's commands, then, pretty clearly, it's not *dependent* on those commands and the Divine Command Theory of Morality does no significant work for us—doesn't really tell us what morality is all about, as it purports to do. But from these three premises a conclusion clearly follows, and follows deductively:

The Divine Command Theory of Morality fails.

For *either way* it fails, and *one* of those ways *has* to be accepted by the Divine Command theorist. Whether right or wrong, this is a beautiful argument.

Logic also tells us about lots of common mistakes in reasoning—called "fallacies"—which can prevent an argument from being logically correct, let alone warranting the label "beautiful." Careful reasoners will want to know about them. For example, suppose that after some discussion Joe's atheist friend Terri agrees with him that "If God exists then life is meaningful." Joe may think: "Aha! I can just add the premise that life *is* meaningful and then I'll be able to show Terri she has to draw the conclusion that God exists!" But this idea rests on a simple fallacy, which involves Joe confusing his actual first premise "If God exists then life is meaningful" with a premise that turns what it says around: "If life is meaningful then God exists." Easy to do, and important to avoid.

Seeing that Terri would *have* to turn Joe's first premise around in this way, in order logically to deduce the conclusion that God exists in this case, is a significant insight. But of more general importance is learning a certain sensitivity to the complex inner structure of such "If/then" propositions, which logicians call conditional propositions or *conditionals* since they say that the truth of one proposition is a condition for that of another. This inner structure has consequences for what can and cannot be done with conditionals in reasoning. Formal logic is the study of precisely such things.

We can display the inner structure of a conditional in the following way: If P then Q. As the "P" and the "Q" help us to express, a conditional proposition is really two distinguishable propositions stuck together by means of "if" and "then." This is its inner structure. Take again the conditional "If God exists then life is meaningful." After the "if" comes one proposition: *God exists*. And after the "then" comes another: *Life is meaningful*. The conditional doesn't say that either of these propositions is true. In fact, the conditional could be true even if both are false. All the conditional says is that *if* the first proposition is true, *then* the second is also true. The conditional is about the *connection* between those two, and its complex inner structure is required to express that connection. But mind your Ps and Qs! Get the structure turned around and you have errors like that of Joe, mentioned a couple of paragraphs back.

Now even though such conditionals alone may not help us reach any interesting conclusions, their inner structure often lends itself to powerful reasoning that goes far indeed. This happens when a conditional is clearly true and when, in an argument, we can *add* to it a *second* premise that is also clearly true and does either of two things: affirms the "P" proposition, or denies the "Q" proposition. Using the clearly true God conditional "If God exists then life is meaningful" to illustrate, we could build such an argument if it were also clearly true that God exists, or else also clearly true that life is not meaningful. In the first case we would have this argument (I have displayed its logical "skeleton" alongside):

If God exists then life is meaningful.	If P then Q
God exists.	P
Life is meaningful.	Q

And in the second case we would have this argument:

If God exists then life is meaningful.	If P then Q
Life is not meaningful.	Not-Q
God does not exist.	Not-P

Either way we get a conclusion (the third statement) that follows with necessity from the first two statements taken together. In both cases, if the premises are true, the conclusion *must* be true too. So the conditional alone may be weak, even if true, but if it keeps such company, and the company can be seen to be true too, then it becomes powerful indeed—helping to deliver us a conclusion we *must* accept if we don't want to be illogical.

Unfortunately, in both of the cases just mentioned, we have the conditional in the first premise keeping company with an untrustworthy partner in the second. It is not at all obviously true that God exists, or that life is not meaningful. This may help to explain why Joe, when talking to Terri, instead latched onto the proposition *Life is meaningful*, which most of us would accept without hesitation. But using that as the second premise yields only the logical fallacy mentioned earlier:

If God exists then life is meaningful.	If P then Q
Life is meaningful.	Q
God exists.	P

Why is this conditional argument fallacious and the others not? Just inspecting it for a while may tell you. It's all about that "If/then" structure. When you say that if God exists then life is meaningful you are saying two things. One is that God's existence is enough—*sufficient*—for life to be meaningful. As logicians put it: P is a sufficient condition for Q. This is why if we add, as in the first conditional argument above, that God *does* exist, it follows that life is meaningful. It has to be. If P is sufficient for Q and you've got P, well, then you've got Q! The other thing the conditional in question says is that life being meaningful is unavoidably bound up with—*necessarily comes with*—God's existence. Q is a *necessary* condition for P. (Notice that the order of "P" and "Q" is reversed here.) This is why if we add, as in the *second* conditional argument above, that life is *not* meaningful, it follows that God does *not* exist. This must then be so. If Q is necessary for P and you don't have Q, well, then you don't have P! But in the third conditional argument the second premise doesn't tell us either that something *sufficient* for life to be meaningful *is* the case or that something *necessary* for God to exist *isn't*: it tells us only that something *necessary* for God to exist *is* the case. And that could be true even if something *else* that is necessary for God to exist is *not* the case. So it doesn't logically follow in this case that God exists. If Q is necessary for P and you've got Q, well, you still might not have P!

We can use another conditional to illustrate: *If John won the race then John entered the race.* This is true enough, and so if you know that John won the race in question—something that would never happen if the John in question is the author of this book—you can logically conclude that he entered it, and if you know that he didn't enter it, you will logically conclude that he didn't win it. (These two bits of reasoning mimic the first two God-related conditional arguments above.) But now suppose all you know is that he *did* enter the race. Entering is certainly *necessary* for winning, but much else is necessary too! And so even if you know it to be true that *if John won the race then John entered the race* and know also that *John entered the race*, it would be quite illogical for you to conclude from those two pieces of information that *John won the race*. Seeing this, you can also see why Joe's argument to Terri is fallacious: indeed, *any* argument having the form "If P then Q, Q, therefore, P" is fallacious. This is what logic tells us.

One further instance of what logic tells us will also be instructive later in the book, when we reveal the inner structure of the hiddenness argument. It too concerns conditionals, and it will allow us to use what we've learned about the structure *if P then* Q to take things just a little further. For it is about how a first premise having this structure can be followed by a second having the *same* structure, and how those two can deductively lead to a conclusion that is *also* a conditional. (Now we're really talking about a conditional argument! In this sort of argument *all* the propositions are conditionals.) In such an argument the conclusion follows because of how the three conditionals, in virtue of their form, *hook together*.

Of course the three conditionals in such an argument don't all say exactly the same thing—that would make for a deductively valid but rather boring argument. Their content is different. And so to display the structure here—to show the different partners in this dance of logic—we can't stick to "P" and "Q." We want to go further down the alphabet and include "R." And we'll do so by showing how Q is hooked up with R. *If P then* Q is the logical skeleton of the first premise, and *If* Q *then* R is the second; and those two logically take us to the third step in the dance: *If P then* R. It looks like this:

If P then Q
If Q then R
If P then R

Recall what I said earlier about P's *sufficiency* for Q and Q's *necessity* for P in any conditional proposition. The first premise here says that P is sufficient for Q. The second premise starts where the first left off and takes things a step further, saying that Q, just referred to, is sufficient for R. And *that* logically allows us to say—indeed *requires* us to say—that *P* is sufficient for R. If a first thing is enough to get you a second, and the second a third, well, then the *first* thing just got you the third. The idea is really quite simple, even though it takes a lot of words to express it. (And now you see why logicians use symbols!) Let's put some bodies on those skeletons and illustrate with a real live argument—I've put brackets around the statements taking the place of P, Q, and R:

If [our company won the contract] then [the manager is happy].
If [the manager is happy] then [the manager is smiling].
If [our company won the contract] then [the manager is smiling].

Logic tells us that if the first two of these propositions are true, then the third must be true too. And, again, it's all about the inner structure of those conditional propositions.

But why, you ask, would we want to make such an argument, with a conclusion that is *still just a conditional*—a proposition that, as we saw earlier, is of a sort that can't do much intellectual work on its own? Well, some arguments are really *chains* of reasoning, containing several such moves from premise(s) to conclusion, one following another. And it's not hard to see how our conditional conclusion here would be useful if you happen to have a position in the company referred to and, having detected the manager crying in the bathroom, are now able to add this premise: "The manager is *not* smiling." The conditional conclusion together with this extra premise has the logical skeleton *"If P then R, and not-R,"* from which, by a principle mentioned earlier, it follows that *not-P*. Or, adding the relevant body part, it follows that *Our company didn't win the contract*—a perhaps useful, if depressing, piece of information.

Truth

But logic won't tell you *everything* you need to know in order to evaluate an argument for the truth of some fundamental proposition such as the proposition that we have free will or that God exists. The writers of those old *Star Trek* episodes in which Spock claims to be governed entirely by logic didn't understand this. Governed by logic alone, Spock would know when Kirk's conclusion follows from his premises and when it doesn't, but he might have no way at all of determining whether Kirk's premises are true. Talk about an intellectual handicap!

And so if Kirk says that Spock shouldn't drink from a certain glass since it contains Romulan ale and all the Romulan ale on board has been poisoned, Spock, knowing only logic, would be able to see that *if* Kirk's premises are true his conclusion (that Spock shouldn't drink from that glass) is going to be true too. But he wouldn't yet know whether Kirk's premises *are* true. And that would make it rather hard, to say the least, for him to know what to do (or not do).

To know whether an argument, a specimen of reasoning, is a *good one all things considered*, you pretty clearly need to know both these things, both whether it is logically correct and whether its premises are true. Now, it can often be hard to tell whether this is the case. In particular, it can be hard to tell whether the premises of an argument are true—in a way, logic is the easy part—even though good arguers will try to use as premises propositions that the members of their audience will see they already have reason to accept. And so if he is a good reasoner and not just a great logician, Spock, hoping to get Kirk to conclude that his claim that *All the Romulan ale on board has been poisoned* is questionable, will find the idea of including among his premises the insulting but true claims that Kirk is gullible and that Kirk often jumps to conclusions less appealing than the idea of including such true premises as that he, Spock, has already drunk from his glass and is fine and that Vulcans don't lie about such matters.

But when you *do* know *both* that an argument is logically correct *and* that it has true premises—when both logic and truth are on your side—then you have everything you need. You are off to the races, intellectually. Then you can say that the argument is in every way impeccable and that people ought to be convinced by it. For now you have premises which can be seen to be true, and a conclusion which has to be true if they are—which *follows* from them on the iron rails of logic. Voilà! Our knowledge has just taken a step forward.

"From"

Understanding arguments better in this way will help you understand what philosophers mean when they speak of an argument "from" this or that. In philosophical work concerning religion, for example, we have on the side of atheism (which denies the existence of a person-like God) the argument *from* evil and also the argument *from* hiddenness. On the side of theism, we have the argument *from* miracles and the argument *from* religious experience. What is that word "from" doing there, you may ask. (This is just what another non-philosopher friend of mine *did* delicately ask me once after reading some of my work, thinking that I'd made a grammatical mistake.) Well, the answer is that what we see here is just a way of identifying—labeling—arguments by reference to the sort of *premise* that is most dominant in them. If you produce an argument, you've decided you want to travel, intellectually. You mean to go *from* someplace—namely, your premises—*to* another place—namely, your conclusion. The argument from evil moves from alleged facts about evil to the conclusion that God does not exist. The argument from miracles opposes this conclusion on the basis of alleged facts about miracles. No grammatical error. Just a bit of technobabble!

Since reasoning about fundamental matters is very challenging, philosophers emphasize extreme clarity. This explains why they'll often set out their reasoning with numbered propositions, indicating in some way which are the premises and which are conclusions—for example, by using that word “from.” Three of the arguments we’ve encountered can be used to illustrate as we conclude this chapter (I’ve revised the first one a bit for maximum clarity):

Argument I

(1) Either right actions are right because God commands them, or God commands them because they are right.
(2) If the first option is correct then morality is arbitrary, and if the second is correct then it is autonomous.
(3) One of the two options has to be correct.
(4) Both options are fatal to the Divine Command Theory of Morality.
(5) The Divine Command Theory of Morality fails (from 1–4).

Argument II

(1) If God exists then life is meaningful.
(2) God exists.
(3) Life is meaningful (from 1 and 2).

Argument III

(1) If God exists then life is meaningful.
(2) Life is not meaningful.
(3) God does not exist (from 1 and 2).

And it will be useful to notice again, in relation to the second and third of these arguments, how important it is to choose premises that members of your audience can see are true!

CHAPTER 2

A CONCEPTUAL MAP

Continuing with our theme of explaining what philosophers are up to when they produce what looks like technobabble, but moving closer to the particular concepts of this book, let's now think a bit about that term "hiddenness" and why it has come to be employed. And let's also make some of the connections among concepts that will be required to see just what we're talking about when, in our subsequent discussion of hiddenness, we refer to arguments for or against the existence of a being called "God."

Hiddenness

Theologians have long spoken of the hiddenness of God. There's even talk of it in the Bible and in other religious scriptures. So religious people might be forgiven for finding it odd that the hiddenness of God should be regarded as a basis for atheism. Philosophers, too, might think this odd since on the most natural interpretation, being hidden means that, however indiscernibly, what's hidden exists. (Think of the hidden locket or your mother's hidden fear that you don't love her—it can't be hidden unless it exists.) With your brain sharpened by the previous chapter, you'll be inclined to ask this question: How could it follow from the claim that God is hidden, which implies that God *exists,* that God does *not* exist?

One way of trying to make sense of what's going on here involves seeing how someone might object to what the theologians are saying while still quite naturally using their language to do so. Hiddenness reasoning in support of atheism arises when someone looks at facts in the world interpreted by the religious in terms of God's hiddenness (for example, conditions sustaining religious nonbelief—more on this in a moment) and says: "I don't think these facts would *be* facts if there were a God." Given the context as set by theology, it is natural for the arguer to say: God would not be hidden *in this way*. By the same token it is natural to speak of the relevant sort of divine hiddenness as a problem and of any atheistic argument exploiting this problem as an argument from divine hiddenness, when what people really have in mind is again *those facts*, which *would* hide God in a certain way if there were a God. When atheists say or imply that God is hidden, therefore, what they should be taken to mean is that the world contains such facts.

It was because of issues like these that when I set out to develop the argument that is now called the hiddenness argument, I actually tried to avoid applying to it any such label. Instead I wanted to call it the argument from reasonable nonbelief (by which I meant inculpable or blameless nonbelief), and thus refer directly to the facts I found problematic. I also had some trouble deciding on a name for the book in which I developed the argument—"hiddenness" kept cropping up and I kept reminding my editor that a problem of divine hiddenness could really literally exist only for people who believed in God. We went around and around on this for a while, and finally I phoned my undergraduate mentor Terence Penelhum, with whom I had stayed in touch, to see if he could help. His suggestion, offered without a second's delay, was perfect: *Divine Hiddenness and Human Reason*. I immediately saw how this described the book: human reason would here *test* the notion that a God would be hidden in such a way as to make nonbelief inculpable.

But this choice of title, combined with the complex linguistic and conceptual issues lurking here and a certain allure in the word "hiddenness," ensured that the word kept coming back; other people used it when identifying my argument even though I myself had hoped not to do so. The word is attractive in some way—colorful and a bit mysterious, perhaps—while "inculpable nonbelief" sounds plodding and awkward and downright boring. And then there's the fact that what I described in the argument's premises would indeed amount quite literally to the hiddenness of God *if God existed*—which of course my theistic critics believed to be the case. In their view, God really was hiding or hidden from us, and they were trying to explain why. So how could they be mistaken in calling what I was talking about the hiddenness of God?

I ended up giving in. As I saw it, I would tolerate "the argument from hiddenness" or "the argument from divine hiddenness" so long as everyone acknowledged that the expression, when employed by a nonbeliever like me, was being used in a decidedly *non-literal* sense, as a way of talking about facts that would hide God were there to be a God—facts that could be given a neutral description (e.g., "the inculpability of much nonbelief") and accepted as belonging to the world in which we live by theist and atheist alike. And I myself would call the argument *the hiddenness argument* instead of "the argument from divine hiddenness"—a practice which seemed to me to avoid the most glaringly problematic connotations. Since I called it that, many others came to do so too.

So that's the story of how the hiddenness argument got its name. In this book, the word "hiddenness" will sometimes carry a non-literal sense, as when the argument itself is named, and sometimes a literal one, as when we consider religious accounts or explanations of the troubling phenomenon to which the argument refers, which are given in terms of God actually hiding or being hidden from us.

But what exactly is this phenomenon, already identified as related to nonbelief in some way, that the hiddenness argument finds problematic and indeed incompatible with the existence of God? What is it that the hiddenness argument, in its non-literal way, will call "hiddenness" or "divine hiddenness" and its critics often think the result of a literal hiddenness of God? To some extent, the answer will have to await our fuller discussion of the argument in subsequent chapters. But there are a couple of things I want to say right here, where my aim is to prepare us for that discussion.

First, please do notice that there are all kinds of ways in which facts about God might be hidden from us even if God's *existence*—with which the argument is alone concerned—were not hidden. So whether we take the term literally or non-literally, "hiddenness" in connection with the hiddenness argument will always refer to a *narrow slice* of what theologians and others have meant to express by means of it. Someone who's pretty sure God exists might still wonder, for example, why God's nature—who God is in God's heart of hearts—is less than clear. She might wonder why God's plans for the world are unknown to her. Or she might wonder why God isn't consistently available to her experience. The hiddenness argument does not address any of *these* things.

Second, the hiddenness phenomenon, unlike the fact of evil, isn't best thought of as something we can easily and naturally identify out in the world, just like that, and then argue about—here's x: would God permit it or not? Not many people talk this way about inculpable nonbelief! When I set out to develop the argument, I realized that to do a decent job philosophically I needed to ground it in general and "ungiveuppable" facts about the nature of any person-like God there may be (anything else might have been dismissed as expressing personal idiosyncrasy or late twentieth-century prejudice). So, while recognizing that I was concerned in some way with how easy it is, even for conscientious philosophers, not to believe in God, I wanted to start by thinking about general properties or characteristics of a God such as justice or love *to see what relevant points might emerge from such reflection.* I came to think of this as starting "from above" (with abstract reflection on the concept of God) rather than "from below" (with reference to ordinary human experience and common ideas).

Later on we'll see how the argument came to focus first on inculpable or blameless nonbelief and then, more specifically, on nonresistant nonbelief (nonbelief that doesn't arise from any resistance toward God on the part of the nonbeliever). "Divine hiddenness" in its non-literal sense is, for the argument, just the fact that there are in the world such phenomena as these. As you can see, nonresistant nonbelief isn't the sort of thing that will immediately jump out at you when you scan the world and think about whether there is a God. But it *is* something that jumps out at you after you've engaged in a certain sort of reflection on the nature of God.

Ultimism

Now *there's* a word you won't bump into in ordinary life! But notice that it's linguistically reminiscent—and intentionally so—of a much more common word: "theism." The word "theism" means "belief in God" or "the claim that God exists," where "God" is assumed to name a religious reality. (For those who might be wondering, this is why I would not regard deism as a form of theism: deism's creator doesn't care enough about us to play any religious role.) This word "theism," as I say, is commonly used and handy. But a word was needed for the more general idea of an ultimate divine or religious reality, of which theism's idea of a personal God is an elaboration. When I looked for one I found only a blank space. Sure, there's "supernaturalism," but that word is too broad: lots of things might be supernatural without having any religious relevance (the ghosts knocking about in your attic, for example). In 2003 I chose the word "ultimism" to fill the empty space.

Ultimism, more precisely, is the general claim that there is a reality ultimate in three ways: in the nature of things (metaphysically), in inherent value (axiologically), and in its importance for our lives (soteriologically). And that's *all* it says: nothing more specifically about such things as love or knowledge or personal power will be found in it. Now before getting a bit further into what those long -lly words in parentheses mean, let's linger a bit over the word "ultimate." From contexts of ordinary life one can tell that to be ultimate is to be deepest or greatest or best, and to be so in a sense deserving a number of exclamation marks: the ultimate car or meal or partner in life is more like the greatest *possible*!! "Ultimate" takes us to the very limit of whatever it adjectivizes.

Clearly we can also talk about what's ultimate in the universe, and here the word is being used a bit differently, without bringing value into it. Even scientists could—and do—ask about what's ultimate in the universe, meaning something like "What's the ultimate *fact*?" When a physicist such as Stephen Hawking tells you his latest proposal as to the proper contents of the Theory of Everything, he's speaking about what's ultimate in this sense. Thinking that the physical universe (or multiverse) exhausts reality, many physicists really do mean the theory of *everything*. Philosophers will here speak of what is the deepest or most fundamental fact about the nature of reality—what, for example, is the fact (if there is one) in terms of which everything else is properly explained?

Since the study of such things in philosophy is called metaphysics, it's only a short step from here to an understanding of the concept of something *metaphysically ultimate*. A metaphysically ultimate reality, as I use the term, is something whose existence is the ultimate or most fundamental fact about the nature of things, in terms of which any other fact about what things exist and how they exist would have to be explained in a comprehensive and correct account. Plato, in speaking of the form of the Good, just like Hawking in reference to the elusive Theory of Everything, had in mind something bearing metaphysical ultimacy in this sense. Religious people tend to have it in mind too. That's why I include metaphysical ultimacy as one property that an ultimate divine reality would possess—one property needed for the truth of ultimism.

But it's not the only one. As a physicist you might think you had discovered the final theory of physics, but you wouldn't count as an ultimist and as religious unless certain further conditions were satisfied. In particular, we need to bring *value* back into the picture. What the average religious person regards as metaphysically ultimate (obviously without using that terminology), whether it be God or some other thing, she also regards as embodying the deepest possible value. The medieval philosopher and theologian Anselm of Bec, before he became Anselm, Archbishop of Canterbury, famously spoke of the divine as that-than-which-a-greater-cannot-be-thought. (In the second chapter of his *Proslogion,* he spun the famous ontological argument, companion to the cosmological and teleological arguments mentioned in the Preface, out of these words.) A religious reality, in other words, would have to be the *greatest possible* reality, as well as metaphysically ultimate. Since in philosophy the study of value is called axiology, I have dubbed what we see referred to here axiological ultimacy.

The third sort of ultimacy, soteriological ultimacy, is also about value, but in a different way. I've borrowed the word "soteriology" from the Christian tradition, where it's used to mean the study of salvation. Religious salvation, if it ever occurs, is obviously valuable, and uniquely so—it would be valuable *for us.* It would moreover be *ultimately* valuable for us, coming to grips with the deepest facts of human nature and releasing in us whatever is needed for the deepest human fulfillment. Generalizing from this thought, and releasing the words "salvation" and "soteriology" from their Christian moorings, we can think of soteriological ultimacy as possessed by a reality if, in relation to that reality, the deepest or ultimate human good can be attained. It's natural here to think of the unsurpassable greatness of the divine—axiological ultimacy—being in some way communicated or channeled to us and, at least in the most generous religious understandings, through us to the rest of the world.

So why are we talking about all this, you may say. Weren't we supposed to be talking about *God*? Well, in a way we still are. My claim is that the idea of God, which (as we've left implicit until now) is in western philosophy the fairly specific and detailed idea of *an all-powerful, all-knowing, all-good and all-loving creator of the universe,* represents *one way* in which the *broader* idea of ultimism can be filled out, a way that utilizes the concept of a person. Theism gives to ultimism a face, one might say (quite a familiar one). Another way of putting it is to say that theism is an elaborated or personal *version* of ultimism. You could also turn the point into an equation: theism = personal ultimism.

This all suggests, of course, that there might be other elaborations of ultimism, and in fact there are. You'll find them in non-Christian and non-theistic religious traditions of the world, such as Theravada Buddhism or Advaita Vedanta, a form of Hinduism. There may indeed be many ways of filling out the general ultimistic picture that we humans—a rather early manifestation of intelligence and spiritual sensitivity on our planet—haven't yet thought of. In some of them personhood as we know it may play no role at all; in others it may be subsidiary to (for us) unknown higher realities. That is why ultimism seems to me to make a better framework for religious reflection than theism, which develops its entire understanding of the divine from the idea of personhood.

So what's the moral of the story? Well, one moral is this: that the hiddenness argument is an argument against the existence of *God* (or against the truth of theism), not an argument against the existence of what ultimism refers to. Properly conceived, within a philosophical context, the hiddenness argument will be viewed as a way of testing whether the most common elaboration of ultimism in the world today, the idea of a person-like God (a particular being and center of consciousness with power, knowledge, goodness, and love that can be understood by extrapolation from our own similar attributes plus ultimization), can rationally survive. Saying that it can't survive is quite consistent with supposing that some other version of ultimism is or may be true. The historical Buddha, Siddhartha Gautama, can be seen as having done just that. So we have this interesting result: one can quite consistently be an atheist and an ultimist at the same time. Or, at least, if we use the word "atheist" in the way that it has almost always been used in the history of western philosophy, we'll see things that way.

This may seem surprising to some readers, who have become used to thinking of atheists as denying *all* religious claims. It has to be conceded that what we might call popular atheism often does so, but this, I'm inclined to believe, is often due to unclear thinking, a tendency to blur concepts at their edges or run them together—for example, the concept of atheism and that of metaphysical *naturalism*, the idea that physical nature is all there is. The latter idea *is* perfectly irreligious but the former is not. An atheist in the philosophical sense need not be a metaphysical naturalist, and the basic resources for understanding I have introduced in this chapter and in the previous one will help you see why, for they will help you see that from the denial of a personal God it simply does not follow that one is claiming to be false *every* way in which nature could be less than all there is.

This is an important insight. Perhaps "technobabble" has its uses!

CHAPTER 3

WHY SO LATE TO THE SHOW?

People like to say there are no original ideas. I dislike this idea because it's so unoriginal. In my view there are plenty of original ideas—though of course it may be that not all of the parts of an original idea (should it have parts) are brand new. And I think a great many more original ideas may be found far down the road in science and philosophy, because intelligence on our planet might have miles to go before it sleeps.

So is the hiddenness argument original? I'm probably giving that impression when in my subtitle I call it "philosophy's new challenge to belief in God." Here we need to make a distinction already suggested in the Preface, between the germ of an idea and its development. The idea that weak evidence for the existence of God or the presence of nonbelief might count against the truth of theism does appear here and there in the history of philosophy—though quite rarely. But it took until 1993 for it to be fully developed into an explicit argument against the existence of God. And this argument is, I believe, original. (I'm not alone in saying so: my critics in philosophy have done the same.)

However in this chapter I am much less interested in pursuing the questions whether and how the hiddenness argument is original than in a somewhat different question, which would be worth pursuing even if that argument were not original. Why is it only *now* that we're seriously discussing, in philosophy, the issues raised by the hiddenness argument? In calling the hiddenness argument "philosophy's new challenge to belief in God" we may have in mind not only the originality of the argument but also *the fact that it has recently been gathering steam in philosophy*. A challenge wouldn't really count as "philosophy's new challenge" unless it had received wide attention and come to be widely discussed alongside other theistic and atheistic arguments. This is now happening for the hiddenness argument. But why did it take so long for such a thing to occur? Where was the hiddenness argument during all of philosophy's history?

By considering this issue we'll be able to get out into the open and at least preliminarily deal with some of the basic issues that meet here in a way that will be useful later on. We'll also be able to at least gesture at certain other directions discussion might have gone when the possibility of a hiddenness argument started to come into focus—and might still go in the future.

Precursors

Let's begin by identifying those times in philosophical history when what I've called the "germ" of the idea of hiddenness did make an appearance. Then, in the following sections, we can think about why the discussion never went anywhere.

The most conspicuous examples appear from the seventeenth century on. There is first of all some relevant evidence in the writings of the French polymath and mathematical genius Blaise Pascal, who toward the end of his short life in the 1600s, plagued by illness, put a lot of thoughts about the hiddenness of God (literally construed) into his *Pensées*, spending a good deal of his precious remaining time puzzling over why the existence of God and the truth of Christian claims should frequently seem obscure.

Pascal recognized that the French *philosophes*, whose casual approach to things religious he disdained, were inclined to turn such obscurity into an objection to Christianity. But the fragmented nature of his work, which he didn't live to complete, is such that it isn't clear whether he took them to be saying that this obscurity is a reason to *disbelieve* or simply that it means there isn't sufficient reason to *believe*. "'If I had seen a miracle,' they say, 'I should be converted'," we read in one place. In another, again with reference to Christianity's cultured detractors, we read the following: "If this religion boasted that it had a clear sight of God and plain and manifest evidence of his existence, it would be an effective objection to say that there is nothing to be seen in the world which proves him so obviously." The "effective objection" here is apparently an objection not to the existence of God but to the idea that belief in God's existence is obviously and well supported.

So whether an argument from obscurity *for atheism* is suggested in Pascal is itself obscure. But as to Pascal himself we can say this: though he appears to have had his own dalliances with doubt, it generally seemed obvious to him that Christianity actually proclaims a hidden God who may choose to be revealed only when one seeks for God with all one's heart, and also that those who complain of obscurity in the way the *philosophes* do haven't come close to fulfilling this condition. Some contemporary responses to the hiddenness argument, as we will see, borrow from this way of thinking.

Moving on to the eighteenth century we find a tantalizing suggestion of something like hiddenness reasoning in the work of the English philosopher Joseph Butler. In his greatest book, *The Analogy of Religion*, which quite impressed his Scottish contemporary David Hume, Butler at one point puts the problem with which he's concerned in the following way: "If the evidence of revelation appears doubtful, this itself turns into a positive argument against it, because it cannot be supposed that, if it were true, it would be left to subsist upon doubtful evidence."

Butler is concerned about the truth of Christian claims; the existence of God he thinks is made clear enough by certain rational arguments, such as the teleological argument. But trade his focus for that of the hiddenness argument and you have an intriguing suggestion of how to argue against the existence of God: when the evidence for God is inconclusive, *this itself* should be taken as a conclusive reason for disbelief, because God would never allow the evidence to be thus inconclusive. In other words, there's no logical room for agnosticism; seeing what makes her agnostic, the agnostic should be led by it straight past agnosticism to atheism.

What Butler says here is, as far as I know, the earliest clear case of such reasoning in the history of philosophy. The very same sort of reasoning occurred to me when, in my twenties and studying at the University of Calgary in Alberta, Canada, I began thinking about hiddenness issues. This experience started a train of thought that, while doing a doctorate in philosophy at Oxford, brought me finally to the hiddenness argument. It was while investigating this experience that I discovered Butler had reached the germ of my thinking before me. But neither he nor anyone else had developed the idea, and neither in its Christian form nor in the more general form that spoke to my concerns had it ever made so much as a dent on philosophical discussion.

Come with me now to the nineteenth century, where we find the German philosopher Friedrich Nietzsche fuming about Christian belief, including belief in a personal God of love and kindness. In one brilliant episode, penned before the madness that would eventually engulf him, Nietzsche asks some penetrating questions: "A god who is all-knowing and all-powerful and who does not even make sure his creatures understand his intentions—could that be a god of goodness? Who allows countless doubts and dubieties to persist, for thousands of years, as though the salvation of mankind were unaffected by them, and who on the other hand holds out frightful consequences if any mistake is made as to the nature of truth? Would he not be a cruel god if he possessed the truth and could behold mankind miserably tormenting itself over the truth?"

Here something like the hiddenness problem is suggested, though notice that Nietzsche speaks of the hidden "intentions" of God rather than of God's hidden existence; no doubt it would only require a small adjustment to fix that. More importantly, Nietzsche focuses on the pain of religious doubt when he (very briefly) considers why we might not expect God to be hidden. As we'll see in the section "Evil?," this invites an assimilation of hiddenness to the problem of evil that is far too quick. In any case, Nietzsche's argument didn't go anywhere either.

Finally, we come to the century just past, which along with everything else includes a few comments or remarks that might be thought redolent of hiddenness concerns. A number of these are much less obviously capable of being pressed into service here than has sometimes been thought. Consider, for example, the English philosopher Bertrand Russell's famous answer to the question of what he would say were he to meet God after a lifetime of nonbelief. There are various versions of the story, but the answer was apparently along the lines of "Not enough evidence, God, not enough evidence!" This answer affords God an explanation as to why Russell never *believed*; it doesn't contain even the germ of an argument that a real God would have provided more evidence, an argument which Russell could have put forward as justifying *dis*belief. The situation here is similar to the one I mentioned earlier in connection with Pascal's *philosophes*.

The same holds for a remark made by the philosopher of science N. R. Hanson, who said this: "There is no single natural happening, nor any constellation of such happenings, which establishes God's existence.... If the heavens cracked open and [a] Zeus-like figure... made his presence and nature known to the world, *that* would establish such a happening." It may appear that, according to Hanson, the absence of such happenings in some way proves that God does not exist. But I interpret him as saying, much more modestly, that God's existence *could* be established; perhaps that he (Hanson) *would* believe if such events occurred; and maybe also that something like this would *need* to occur in order for him to believe. Again, not even the germ of a hiddenness argument for atheism here.

But there is one in an interesting twentieth-century essay by the British philosopher Ronald Hepburn, who pretty much reproduces Butler's form of reasoning (though this time we do have a reference to God's existence and not just the truth of Christian revelation), adding a healthy dab of Nietzsche: "One might be tempted to see in... [ambivalent evidence] a vindication of atheism. For how could such an ambiguous universe be the work of perfect love and perfect power? Could this be a way to love and express love, to leave the loved one in bewildering uncertainty over the very existence of the allegedly loving God? Would we not have here a refined weapon of psychological torture? That is: if the situation is ambivalent, it is *not* ambivalent, since its ambivalence is a conclusive argument against the existence of the Christian God." And another clear hint of hiddenness appeared a few decades later in a paper by George Schlesinger called "The Availability of Evidence in Support of Religious Belief." According to Schlesinger, a perfectly *just* God would distribute evidence of God's existence *evenly*, so that the opportunity to believe in God and experience the benefits of belief was missed by no one.

In talking about "religious ambiguity" during the twentieth century, Hepburn was joined by John Hick and my own teacher, Terence Penelhum. It was in thinking about Penelhum's work on religious ambiguity that, as mentioned earlier, I came to ask whether the claim that the world is religiously ambiguous, a sort of summarizing proposition about religious evidence, might itself be evidence—and indeed disambiguating evidence—against the existence of God. Later I saw Butler had had the same idea. Later still I found it in Hepburn, and also came upon Schlesinger's related idea. But I found such ideas clearly stated by no one else. And certainly no one had thoroughly developed the argument lurking here. No, as the twentieth century drew to a close, the hiddenness argument for all practical purposes remained hidden.

So we have this question: Why did nothing like the hiddenness argument ever succeed in getting off the ground before I decided to go to bat for it?

Evil?

One possible answer is that no one ever clearly noticed—or at least no one managed to get the ball rolling on—the relationship between any of these precursor thoughts and *the problem of evil*. If they had done so, it may be said, the hiddenness problem would naturally have been developed as one part of the problem of evil, which has always been well known and deemed important. Those who say this sort of thing emphasize that philosophers use the word "evil" very broadly, to refer to anything bad. And surely, they suggest, hiddenness (or whatever phenomenon of nonbelief we have in mind when uttering that word) *is* bad, even if an unusual form of badness—an intellectual form of badness—that could easily be overlooked or neglected. George Schlesinger, for example, one of our "precursors," seems implicitly to suggest this approach by calling a certain sort of nonbelief unjust, though no one else picked up his idea and ran with it.

Look closely at the vital premise here: hiddenness is bad. Is that premise true? You may notice pretty quickly that not everyone is going to deplore nonbelief of the sort we've already mentioned. (Atheists or agnostics, for example, might be expected to think it's just the ticket.) And I myself have certainly taken a different direction. Whereas everyone sees that horrific suffering *is* bad, and for the atheist to put forward an argument from evil in the form of an argument from horrific suffering (the most common sort today) is precisely to emphasize the extreme badness of horrific suffering.

But matters are a bit complicated here and the natural comeback is to say that even if the atheist putting forward a hiddenness argument doesn't regard nonbelief as bad, he does need the theist to regard hiddenness as bad—or perhaps someone will want to say that it's part of the atheist's argument that *God* would view hiddenness as bad (if God existed, of course). Thus the hiddenness argument, so it may be said, still reduces to an argument from evil.

This is a tempting view, but like many temptations it should be resisted. Even if a theist actually thinks of the sort of nonbelief I'll be emphasizing as bad (and indeed even if God would do so), we still have to ask—and this is important—*whether it's in virtue of this perceived badness that the atheist expects the theist to find the hiddenness argument persuasive*. And this is not always the case. Moreover, for the hiddenness argument I'll be developing, which, as I've noted, is at the center of debate, it is definitely not the case. And so to try to assimilate the hiddenness discussion that *did* get off the ground to the problem of evil is just a mistake. The hiddenness argument, as we'll see, wants its hearers to be aware that a certain phenomenon of nonbelief is inconsistent with the idea that a God of fullest love exists, and in a manner that could prove convincing even if no one had ever thought of such nonbelief as bad (perfect love, after all, might be expected to do more than just prevent badness). An argument from evil, on the other hand, *has* to say that there are certain things we wouldn't expect from the hand of a benevolent God because they are bad. That's just part of its nature. It follows that the hiddenness argument and the problem of evil are distinct.

Someone might now wonder, in connection with the reference to love, whether we are forgetting the anguish many feel when in doubt about the existence of God, which a loving God would surely be concerned about. Nietzsche, as we have seen, at least suggests this. And Pascal, whom we've also had occasion to consult, spoke for many doubters who came before and after him when (whether from personal experience or empathetically, with others in mind) he said the following: "Seeing too much to deny and not enough to affirm, I am in a pitiful state, where I have wished a hundred times over that, if there is a God supporting nature, she should unequivocally proclaim him." Isn't this just the sort of phenomenon that hiddenness reasoning emphasizes? Didn't Pascal himself characterize the suffering he refers to as the hiddenness of God?

This example provides a good opportunity to underline two points from the previous chapter. There is a difference between divine hiddenness taken literally and hiddenness in the mouth of an atheist. In Pascal we find only the former. Furthermore, although things might no doubt have happened differently, the hiddenness argument of today, as explained in Chapter 2, proceeds "from above" and not "from below;" I had no sure sense going in as to what would be found problematic for theism. And what actually emerged as problematic, as we'll see, is not the anguish of doubt, a common enough concern, but rather the more *general* phenomenon of inculpable or blameless nonbelief. To make the point most pointedly: the hiddenness argument would get along just fine even if no one had ever been wracked by doubt as to the existence of God; blameless nonbelief comes in many forms, not just that one.

So the first answer to this chapter's question about the historical tardiness of the hiddenness argument, which sees it as representing an unremarkable oversight and some unfinished business in connection with the problem of evil, turns out to be less than convincing when inspected with proper care. In particular, the hiddenness argument that is today receiving attention can't be assimilated to the problem of evil. Any attempt to stuff it into that category will find that it continually pops back out.

There is an important moral to this story. It would be a mistake to suppose that the sorts of evil generally treated by philosophers represent a more serious problem than the problem of hiddenness because they are *worse* than any condition of nonbelief. Someone may say, for example, that horrific suffering is unimaginably worse than not being able to believe in God, and so wonder why we're going on about the latter. The hiddenness argument in its very specific emphasis on nonbelief doesn't require nonbelief to be bad *at all*. And which sort of argument is most formidable—the argument from evil or the hiddenness argument—depends entirely on which has access to the most plausible premises and from whose premises the nonexistence of God follows most obviously.

Evolution

I want now to develop briefly what I regard as a better answer to the question why the hiddenness argument was only so recently taken up and taken seriously by philosophers. It's this: the hiddenness argument was waiting for conditions to be right. I don't think conditions *were* right for this challenge to theistic belief to be taken seriously until fairly recently. Several interwoven sorts of cultural evolution had to take place before it could be. I'll mention three.

(i) *Social/psychological evolution*. Today a sensitive awareness of religious diversity is becoming more widely distributed among us. We in the west recognize that there are *non*-western religious beliefs and practices, many of which—for example, many Hindu and Buddhist beliefs and practices—are also non-theistic, having for hundreds or thousands of years been getting along quite nicely without a western picture of divine reality. And we realize that the best of their representatives are typically at least as smart and decent as the best of us. So it's harder even for religious people today to dismiss such individuals as corrupt or misguided than it was, say, for Pascal. We see that there are thoughtful and reflective types who fail to believe in God apparently through no fault of their own. And so if someone suggests that this is the case and God wouldn't allow it, we will listen longer.

There is also, relatedly, a profound secularism among us once quite absent, of a sort finely detailed by Charles Taylor in his doorstop of a book *A Secular Age*. What Taylor finds most striking is how religious faith, once the norm in the west, is now just one option among many. Working within a secular context means that we won't encounter the difficulty intellectuals once had accepting the idea that a person who has nothing wrong with her might fail to believe in God.

At the same time, and especially quite recently, we have experienced a movement toward gender equality and away from certain images that once dominated our social consciousness and reinforced the idea, inherited from religious tradition, of a hidden masculine God: images of the *strong, solitary male* and of the *distant father*. Not so very long ago, no one thought anything of it if a father was absent from the lives of his children for considerable stretches of time, or if he had some trouble relating with them amiably. Indeed, any male who absented himself from ordinary contexts of social interaction to carry out admirable feats on behalf of the "common good" was especially praised. Of course some of these social tendencies remain with us, but they are at the very least severely qualified in an age when men, more commonly than ever before, can be found summoning the strength required to be a stay-at-home dad. And so it is at the very least easier for us to notice and take seriously an argument speaking of God as necessarily loving and thus *open to relationship* with finite creatures.

(ii) *Moral evolution*. The point about love seems to me to have a moral dimension too—though of course moral thinking is done by individuals-in-society. We have come to *value* more a certain relational love which we picture being expressed by men and women alike, or at least to value *less* the "benevolence from a distance" alternative. Moral evolution of this sort is indeed part and parcel of the sorts of social/psychological evolution I have just mentioned; it helps to explain what we now see in the latter realms.

Moral evolution might also be detected in our willingness to grant the existence of conscientious nonbelief. Conscientious *objectors* to belief are almost as uncontroversially real these days as conscientious objectors to war. Here we may see the gradual increase in empathy over the past couple of centuries or so remarked upon by Steven Pinker in his own doorstop *The Better Angels of our Nature*. Empathy can be expected to help us put ourselves in the place of those who tell their stories of honest searching and nonbelief and to make their accounts seem more plausible to us. Ironically, writing nonbelievers off as depraved was in earlier times done from strong moral conviction but is today frequently regarded as being itself morally defective—a matter of imposing on the other an ideological perspective instead of actually getting to know him or her as a person.

(iii) *Philosophical/theological evolution*. All of the sorts of cultural evolution already mentioned appear to be having consequences in philosophy and theology. One sees, in theology, movement away from the picture of God as masculine and father. Even where God is still called father, the father that believers bring to mind is commonly less distant and aloof than he often was for believers in the day of Pascal or of Butler or even of Nietzsche. There appears to be a growing sense that a loving God will have an impulse to behave otherwise, in accordance with the nature of the best *relational* love. Furthermore, the idea that everyone everywhere is corrupt and in a state of resistance toward God is thought even by many theologians to be problematic. In theological quarters the onset of ecumenism and pluralism has reduced such views to an unsavory "cultish" status.

Now some of what I've suggested in my explanation here of why the hiddenness argument had to wait so long for a hearing is admittedly a bit speculative, and of course we'd be unwise to ignore all those who see the changes I have listed as representing a serious fall from grace and who are doing their best to resurrect the old world order. Evolution doesn't necessarily signal improvement, and although many will agree with me that in most of the cases I've mentioned it does amount to improvement, others will disagree. But however they may have arisen, and whether improvements or not, changes evidently *have occurred* in the ways in which investigators of the religious realm think about God and love and nonbelief. And in these altered circumstances, so I suggest, the flourishing in philosophy of a new argument against the existence of God focused on divine hiddenness has became possible.

CHAPTER 4

THE MAIN PREMISE

I grew up in a deeply religious household on the prairie of Manitoba, Canada's "keystone" province (so we self-importantly told each other in school), with a father who, when I was a child, sang me to sleep with songs about Jesus he himself had written. We lived far from any town and were very poor; my dad, though in some ways a startlingly creative individual, suffered from a variety of complexly interwoven physical and mental troubles that undermined his every worldly endeavor. It was left to my mother, a salt of the earth type and my father's opposite, to help us hold body and soul together—and also to my siblings, much older than I, who one by one left home and through ingenuity and grit made a better way in the world, and then supported Mom and Dad and me with the fruits of their labors.

Alone on the prairie with my parents, feeling a loyalty to them and to their God, stirred by what I took to be God's presence in the whirling wind and sky and my inmost thoughts, atheism was unthinkable (I don't believe I even knew the word). I wrote my own songs about Jesus. In three years of Bible and musical training after high school I also sang them (I come from a family of singers). During one year as associate pastor of a Mennonite Church in Alberta I preached the Word as diligently and fervently as anyone. It was only after all this—after I too left home, both literally and metaphorically, discovering all the books about the deeper things of life from which I had been cut off, that religious questions began to arise in me.

They arose quite quickly, as I recall, and although there was considerable pain in letting go of childhood beliefs and experiences at odds with the new insights generated by biblical criticism and philosophical argumentation, and although my loyalties did not shift swiftly, there was also a sheer exhilaration at the *ideas* I found. It was as though they had always been waiting for me, or I for them. And even after the shift occurred, there was still a felt continuity with my previous self, who so earnestly and naively proclaimed to others the "truth" about God. For although I had lost a passel of beliefs, I was still committed to the truth in my newfound vocation as a philosopher. Indeed, an unrelenting and scrupulous pursuit of truth and understanding—a fierce and unwavering desire to know the truth, *whatever* it might be—was something I now set before myself as worthy of cultivation much more consciously and earnestly than I had ever done before.

Ambiguity

One of the ideas that intrigued me in my early days as a nonbeliever (I was not yet a disbeliever), even as it deepened my doubt and thus simultaneously troubled me, was the germ of hiddenness reasoning I mentioned in the previous chapter in connection with the notion of religious ambiguity.

Considering the arguments for and against God's existence and evaluating the intellectual worth of my religious experiences, I at first found myself with just the sense conveyed in the writings of Hick and Penelhum: that the world was somehow religiously ambiguous, equally open to theistic and non-theistic interpretations. When you did your best not to simply impose your own favorite ideas on the discussion, you could see that each side—in fact *multiple* sides—had persuasive ways of making sense of human experience in their own terms and of absorbing objections from the others. Reflecting on this I found my doubt reinforced; although some people seemed able to believe one way or the other despite their recognition of religious ambiguity, I myself couldn't, for I had no idea which view had got it right.

And then came the insight mentioned in the previous chapter, which, although I didn't know it, Butler and Hepburn had had before me: that this fact *itself* might be evidentially significant. If there was good reason for God to prevent religious ambiguity, then this very evidential situation might be *dis*ambiguating, showing that all things considered—that is, with the fact of ambiguity included in the evidence—the world *wasn't* religiously ambiguous but instead spoke clearly against the existence of God.

But what in detail was the argument? My job now was to see exactly what form of reasoning was lurking here and nudge it into the light of day. I tried various avenues which required clarifying the notions of ambiguity and of objective disambiguation in relation to the concepts of evidence and probability, seeking to identify exactly how the relevant ideas should be articulated. But this turned out to be slippery terrain. Was religious ambiguity a matter of swiftly altering patterns in the relevant evidential data? the equal probability of theism and of various atheistic alternatives on available evidence? the relative probability of theism and of those alternatives being objectively indeterminate? . . . The list of possibilities went on and on. The notion of religious ambiguity was itself ambiguous! And although it would have been interesting to explore its various facets, this was not what I had set out to do.

By now I was at Oxford working toward the DPhil in philosophy. And there I realized that I had grabbed hold of the wrong end of the stick. The important thing to take away from the notion of religious ambiguity was not some sophisticated fact or facts about evidence out there in the world articulable by means of probability theory, in which my thesis supervisor, Richard Swinburne, was an expert, but rather simple facts about subjective states of people, such as that *honest doubt about God is possible*. It might even be that objectively the evidence *wasn't* inconclusive because, say, an argument convincingly showing that God exists or very probably exists could be fashioned from existing and available materials, though no one had yet done so. Even if this were to be the case, *still I right now would be in honest doubt*. And I sensed that I would find the argument I was looking for by examining more closely the reasons why a God might not tolerate such a situation.

This is when I decided that I needed to start "from above", motivated by my sense that something was wrong with honest doubt in a theistic universe but letting the argument emerge, taking whatever form it wanted to take, on the basis of some careful thought about the nature of God. What was it about the idea of God that had kept me intellectually troubled by religious ambiguity since I first encountered it? The main premise in this book's formulation of the hiddenness argument, which says nothing about doubt and eventually will be linked to others focused on a much more general conception of nonbelief, still bears the marks of the thinking that followed.

Openness

The hiddenness argument's main premise, stated without analytical fretting or frills and with the aim of maximum intuitive force, is this:

> If a perfectly loving God exists, then there exists a God who is always open to a personal relationship with any finite person.

Let me say right now (especially for the benefit of those who *are* immediately plunged into analytical fretting by such a proposition) that when I say "personal relationship" I mean just what most of us would ordinarily have in mind when using that phrase: a conscious, interactive, and positively meaningful relationship. Notice also that this premise doesn't say that God *would* be perfectly loving. (Of course perfect love is just part of the traditional depiction of God, as I've presented it. But we'll give a hearing to those who think it's a dispensable part in due course.) The premise says only that *if* God is perfectly loving, then a certain something *else* will be true too—something else involving personal relationship. As noted in Chapter 1, logicians call such propositions *conditional* propositions.

We already saw some examples of If/then or conditional propositions back there. One thing we can take from every single one of them is that the truth of what comes after the "if" and before the "then" would be sufficient or *enough* to bring with it the truth of what comes after the "then." So, in this case: the truth of

A perfectly loving God exists

brings with it the truth of

There exists a God who is always open to a personal relationship with any finite person.

Where you have the first thing you'll find the second too. This is what the hiddenness argument's main premise says. Take a look and see whether it strikes you as right. And remember, as you do, that any finite persons there may be will have been *created* by a loving God, if such a God exists.

Of course, having come through Chapter 1, a variety of questions may be buzzing in your head. Here's one: just what *is* this "perfect love" and this "openness" referred to by the premise? Good questions! Having seen, as you probably have, that the premise looks initially plausible, we now need to inspect it more carefully. Otherwise we wouldn't be doing our job as philosophers.

Perfect love, as you may have realized, is here taken to be the best, the greatest, the deepest love that could possibly be realized in God. It's *ultimate* love. Theism is an elaboration of ultimism, the elaboration that says the ultimate reality is a person (a divine one). So if God possesses love at all, then this love must be unsurpassably great—more sublime than that of any mere mortal and indeed expressed in an ultimate way. Such an interpretation I take to be justified and indeed mandated by the wider framework of religious investigation. And even if we can't know everything that perfect love would do or refrain from doing, it may be that we can just see, or that simple arguments can help us see, that it necessarily brings certain things with it. This is like just seeing, as Spielberg's Lincoln suggested we can in the film of that name, the truth of Euclid's "common notion" that "things that are equal to the same thing are equal to each other," or seeing with a bit of thought that, as Euclid also affirms, if $2x = 2y$, then $x = y$. We can see these things even if there are hidden depths of mathematics humans will never penetrate. What we want to know here is whether we can just see that ultimate love would necessarily bring with it openness to personal relationship.

I have already said what I mean by "personal relationship." This is just the general and familiar idea of positively meaningful interaction between persons that they are aware of experiencing. In this connection we should take note of a point that, once noted, will generally remain tacit (unmentioned but understood to apply to this premise). This is that the scope of "finite persons"—the range of individuals to which that phrase refers—is restricted to finite persons *who have the capacities needed for such a relationship*: the capacities of mind and heart needed to be able to be in a meaningful conscious relationship with God, which include such things as a capacity to feel the presence of God, recognizing it as such; a capacity to exhibit attitudes of trust, gratitude, and obedience to God, and so on. (There might be a reason to suppose that, if God existed, more people would have such capacities. But let's not get distracted by this; it would make for a different argument.)

All right. So the premise is saying that if God exists and possesses the greatest possible love, then God will always be open to a meaningful conscious relationship with every finite person capable of participating in it. But what is the relevant openness?

Here we've arrived at the very heart of the argument. I expect you'll have a pretty good intuitive grasp of what is meant by "openness" in this context. But let's look at the term more closely, for this will help to expose the great plausibility of the premise in which it appears. I want, in particular, to underline how thin or *minimal* a notion we've got here.

Openness to relationship, as the argument understands it, doesn't require that God do any particular thing to pursue relationship—suffocating us with attention or even politely asking for it. It's compatible with God standing back, as it were, and giving finite creatures some responsibility for how the relationship will develop or even being experientially elusive when creatures respond presumptuously or complacently. It's compatible with God allowing creatures to close the door to relationship themselves and shut themselves off from God. It doesn't even require that God *want* such relationship, though if perfectly loving, we might expect that something corresponding to this would be realized in God. No, being open in the relevant sense at a certain time simply means *not (then) being closed.* It means *not through one's own actions or omissions making it impossible* for the other, whom one loves, to participate in personal relationship with one at that time should the other wish to do so. Alternatively, and applying this now to God, it means that it will be *possible* for creatures who haven't made it impossible themselves through their own God-obscuring resistance of the divine, to participate in relationship with God; if they want to, they will be able to do so simply by *trying* to do so (notice that this doesn't mean that trying will be easy: perhaps what one would need to do to further a meaningful relationship with God would often be difficult). If thus open to relationship, God sees to it that nothing *God* does or fails to do puts relationship with God out of reach for finite persons at the time in question.

Could our definition of perfect love rightfully be deprived of even so weak a relational condition as is represented by the phrase "always open" when it is taken in this minimal sense? The main premise of the hiddenness argument expects that you will say no. Love is deeply relational. And so how could God at some time count as loving John or Joan as fully and deeply and richly as God can if God at that time is *preventing* John (or Joan) from being able to participate in any way in a meaningful, conscious relationship with God? Such minimal openness as we've identified seems self-evidently to belong to divine love.

To prime your intuition here, imagine that you're listening to your friend, who's describing his parents: "Wow, are they ever great—I wish everyone could have parents like mine, who are so wonderfully loving! Granted, they don't want anything to do with me. They've never been around. Sometimes I find myself looking for them—once, I have to admit, I even called out for them when I was sick—but to no avail. Apparently they aren't open to being in a relationship with me—at least not yet. But it's so good that they love me as much and as beautifully as they do!" If you heard your friend talking like this, you'd think he was seriously confused. And you'd be right. His parents, if your friend's description of them is correct, could certainly be lots of other things—even impressive things, like the best corporate lawyer in the country and the President. They could have set their son up in the best house in town, with money and things galore. But their attitude toward him, whatever it is, doesn't amount to the most admirable love, since they are closed to being in a personal relationship with him.

It may seem, however, that my words "open" and "closed" are getting too much of their power rhetorically. Being "closed" suggests *never* making a personal relationship possible. But such, it may be said, is certainly not the case with God. Even if at a certain time I am unable, just by trying, to participate in relationship with God *then* if I want to, God may still make it possible for me to do things that will give me such an ability in the future. Shouldn't this count as a sort of openness to personal relationship on the part of God?

But for God's attitude toward personal relationship with you *at the time in question* the word "closed" is perfectly appropriate. It's important not to get distracted from this point. And if it is hard to see why consistent openness should be built into our idea of God's unsurpassable love, then it may be worthwhile contemplating a bit the most obviously loving people in our experience. For such people—loving parents, siblings, friends, teachers—consistent openness is taken quite for granted: this is where things *start* in the story of their interaction with us. It seems rather odd for someone to take as a *goal* someone else's openness to personal relationship with them while holding that they are already unsurpassably loving toward them.

Reinforcement

But suppose that after reflection on these points, the openness claim about divine love still doesn't seem self-evident to you, like Euclid's common notion. Maybe we can make it evident with a bit of discussion. First be sure you've distinguished goodness, in the sense of benevolence (a giving disposition), from love. Love entails benevolence but goes beyond it too. For God could be a well-meaning God and perhaps even perfectly good in the sense of benevolent to all finite creatures from a distance, without being open to such relationship as I've mentioned. Whereas what's distinctively wonderful about love, what makes us say that an unsurpassably great person must be loving in a way that goes beyond benevolence, is the desire of a loving person to come close, allowing us explicitly to share in her life. Of course even this is something she might do because of benevolence if we stood to benefit from such relationship, but here it's very important to notice that love values relationship *for its own sake* too. I don't know how many times I've had to correct, in print, the idea that I think a loving God would be open to relationship with us mainly or only because such a relationship would contribute to our well-being. Sure, this might be expected to be a consideration, but it's pretty clearly not the whole of what a loving person will deem important, since otherwise one would be treating loving relationship just as a means to an end, not as an end in itself. If that were your orientation when you love someone, then you'd be prepared to step aside as soon as you thought someone else might be able to make the one you love a bit happier than you can!

So we must be careful to distinguish love from benevolence, remembering that the one who loves values relationship for its own sake. Everyone, no matter how traditional in their theological views, will accordingly be able to agree on at least this much: divine love at *some* time must involve openness to a sharing relationship of the sort we've been talking about. Otherwise it obviously couldn't be the greatest love possible. Moreover, suffering from no limitations of knowledge or power or (therefore) of resourcefulness, an unsurpassably loving God clearly would love finite creatures at *every time* when they exist. Doesn't openness at every time follow?

But something else that might inhibit this realization is the fact that non-ordinary circumstances can be imagined in which *human beings* might be loving *without* openness of the sort in question—at least for a while. Indeed, the benevolence part of love might conceivably come in conflict with the openness-to-relationship part. Contemporary analytical philosophers often enjoy thinking up examples of this kind—*counter*examples to appealing general claims. Here's one that may fit our topic. Suppose Fred, out of a deep love, has been searching for his lost daughter Sally for many years. Today he has finally discovered her whereabouts and he could contact her. But she's right in the middle of a task that cannot be postponed, one in which success is reasonably taken by her as very important; and it's a task that she'd not be able to perform successfully if Fred entered her life just then. Maybe it's interviewing for her dream job or competing in the Olympics or performing a life-saving surgery. So Fred holds off. Now, by doing so he prevents Sally from being able to participate in relationship with him just then, which means he's not open to relationship with her just then. But isn't this kind and even loving of Fred, rather than un-loving?

Similar and perhaps more realistic examples can be imagined—such as the mother who because of a murder conviction has given up her beloved child for adoption, and who later shrinks from revealing herself to the child because she thinks great psychological or social harm for the child may come of it. What such examples suggest is that if we want a principle about love and openness to relationship that is perfectly general and necessarily true, we will need to say something like this: the best love *normally* or *ordinarily* is open to relationship at every moment of its existence. In other words, and a bit more precisely: things should be expected to be so wherever the lover has the resources to accommodate the possible consequences of such openness, making them compatible with the flourishing of both parties and of any relationship that may come to exist between them. And that qualifier "normally" may seem to some to send everything up into the air again, properly leading us back into uncertainty about God and openness.

So let's see what we can do about this misleading "seeming" or appearance. One thing to notice is that the same loving impulse that is our focus entails favoring (seeking, doing what one can to realize) a situation in which what normally is so indeed *is* so. Human love can't always manage this. But precisely because of their love, people like Fred and the mother of our second example would *make* it so, if only they could do so. Fred, for example, while waiting for Sally to finish her task, will mourn the fact that he wasn't able to be there for her from the beginning, getting to know the young woman who now attempts this task and perhaps also helping her with it in some way. And now for the critical point: if God exists as an omnipotent creator and an infinitely rich personal reality, *then God can make it so*. If also unsurpassably loving, God *would* make it so. To make use of the somewhat more precise expression from before: God has the resources to accommodate the possible consequences of openness to relationship with finite persons, making them compatible with the flourishing of all concerned and of any relationship that may come to exist between them.

Yes, you say. But what if there are all sorts of good things God wants to have in the world and can only have by *not* being open to relationship with John or Joan? Who knows what aims God might have that demand at any rate temporary non-openness?

This is a perennial suggestion in discussions like these. But there are two answers that should satisfy us in the present case (at least for now—the issue will come up again).

Remember, to begin, that God gets to set everything up in the first place. So how, if perfectly loving, would God set things up? Add to the picture that God has created finite persons and loves *them* fully. Perhaps God didn't need to create them, but here they are. My question is this: doesn't the fact that God has created persons to love tell us something about the sorts of goods God will pursue in the world we're picturing? If as much content or information as this appears in the idea of a divine reality we are working with, then we *can* know (at least in general terms) what aims will dominate: loving aims. Of course in philosophy it should be an open question whether a God would create at all, given the limitless richness God alone embodies, if God is ultimate. But if we assume that God is a divine person who will create, and will create finite persons, and thus that unlimited and unsurpassable love is to come their way, then in effect we have a statement being made about *what sort of world the actual world shall be.* And this means that we can't any longer shrug our shoulders when some anomalous state of affairs comes along, saying that there might for all we know be goods that justify it.

Here's an analogy. Imagine a single man who marries and has children: Don't these commitments have a transforming effect on the goods he seeks to realize, at least insofar as he is a loving husband and father? Though when he was on his own he spent time with various friends and was otherwise preoccupied with his own wide-ranging pursuits, traveling to far-flung regions of the earth for months at a time, shifting from place to place and from one activity to another, *now* things are different—and quite naturally and rightly so. Now he has a family to help provide for, to support in emotional and financial ways. He can't just take off for Greece or France or Barcelona for long periods at a time to indulge his own interests. Better, he has *new* interests which lead him happily to say no when invitations to do such things arise.

Similarly with God, if God is to be regarded as a loving person—an *ultimately* loving person—who has created vulnerable finite persons to be the object of divine love. The "God" described by those who say that God might, for all we know, choose purposes quite unrelated to finite persons that require God for some time not to be open to relationship with them isn't an ultimately loving being at all. Such a "God" would be comparable to a limited or delinquent father or mother who simply can't or won't live up to the demands taken on board when the commitments of marriage and family are entered into—which is to say, wouldn't be *God* at all.

What follows is that a perfectly loving God in the circumstances we've described would ensure that in the created world all goods God pursues are—as I'll put it—*relationship-compatible* goods. In any world that God creates with finite creatures bearing the relevant capacities, such an impulse must—as we might put it—have "framework" status: other things God does, God chooses to do within a framework or within parameters *that impulse* helps to establish, and the world God creates is, in part, structured by it. Again, God could do something else—God could create a world without finite persons or create no world at all. But any world God creates will be ordered by certain principles, with which some goods are compatible and others may not be. There's nothing surprising or theologically untoward about this. And in the world we're talking about, relational principles will be among them. (Later in the book we'll see how there isn't even any real limitation with respect to the goods God can produce that comes along with this.)

I said there were two preliminary answers to the question about the suggested possibility of goods requiring God to be, at any rate for some time, closed to relationship with finite persons. What's the second? The second is related to the first, and it responds to the idea that it might be out of concern for *us*, for finite creatures, that God is for a time closed to relationship with us, not because of something calling God away to the cosmic equivalent of France or Barcelona. Maybe there's some important good that's good for *us* and requires God to back off. Here's the answer. For any good improving the lives of finite persons that might seem to require God to be for a time closed to relationship with us, there has to be a way for us to achieve that good, or a good of that type, in and perhaps precisely *through* relationship with God. This is again because of the nature of God. If God embodies ultimate value and is the deeper good that every finite good of creaturely life reflects, then no one could better become acquainted with such finite goods than by becoming more fully acquainted, and in a personal way, with God. God doesn't have to make the choice suggested here.

Notice how the alternative view makes both God and relationship with God far too limited and unidimensional. God, by definition, would have to be the greatest possible (richest, deepest, most interesting and most beautiful possible) being, and so getting to know God would take a finite person forever. And in proceeding through the various stages of relationship with God, any of us should expect to encounter versions of the very goods that—according to those who oppose the hiddenness argument—might require God to *prevent* some finite creatures from having access to relationship with God. This must be the case if all goodness is in God. So God doesn't need to prevent anyone from having access to relationship with God in order to procure such goods for us.

What I've said here may still sound a bit abstract, and it is. But it's just what's needed as we begin our discussion of the hiddenness argument to help us see how an objection appealing to possible "greater goods" may be vulnerable. In Chapter 5, when we've seen more of what openness to relationship entails, we'll have a chance to consider against the backdrop we've here constructed specific examples of the goods that are at issue and see exactly how they can be accommodated by the idea of a non-hidden God.

Straws

Reflection on the nature of God, and the reasoning to which it gives rise, therefore may only reinforce the initial impression of plausibility that comes with the main premise of the hiddenness argument. Is there any way at all in which it might still swiftly be rejected by conscientious investigators?

Perhaps someone will suggest that God could be perfectly loving without perpetual openness to relationship if what it is for *God* to be loving is very different from what it is for *us* to be loving. Why should we think that ultimate love would be at all like our love?

The short answer is that it had better be, since otherwise we have no business using that word to refer to it! A somewhat longer one will separate out a way in which the suggestion here is on to something, while showing that this is quite compatible with the concept of love being the very same in the two cases. It is on to something when it is taken as suggesting that how love would be experienced or expressed by a God, or how far it would extend, may well exceed our understanding. What it would *feel like* (to put it crudely) to be God loving, and more generally *what would happen* in God—this might indeed be very different from what we find in any finite human case. But what it *means* to be loving is determined by facts about human language, which link it to giving and sharing and relationship. The concept of love is our concept. There's no escaping this, even in the very phrasing of the suggestion to which I'm responding. For either when one speaks of "what it is for God to be loving" one is referring to our concept of love or not. If so, then of course what I've said applies. If not, then why should we regard the suggestion relevant to our discussion? In that case, who knows what someone who makes that suggestion is talking about?

Here our distinction between theism and ultimism can be helpful. Without the framework concept of ultimism, and more generally without the investigative impulse of the philosopher, which it's intended to assist, it would be easy for our understanding of theism to fade off into absolute mystery, and for theists themselves to take refuge in that region inordinately often during religious discussion. But recognizing that ultimism defines the religious conceptual outer limit, as it were, and that theism *adds* something to this, we can ask *what* it adds. The answer it's natural for philosophers to give, who are used to theism as the claim that there is an all-powerful, all-knowing, all-good, and all-loving creator of the universe, is that it adds *personal* content. That is, theists think of the ultimate reality as a divine person: theirs, as we have seen, is a personal ultimism. The concept of personhood therefore defines what theists bring to the table in philosophy. And this concept is one we have to understand by extrapolation from what we say about ourselves and other beings—for example, in science fiction—as persons. It is in relation to such things that it arose and acquired its distinctive character. In particular, personhood centrally involves such things as consciousness and agency (a capacity to act).

Having seen all this, we see exactly what we're talking about when we address the truth of theism in philosophy, and our investigative agenda is clear. Our job is to see whether *this* way of filling out the idea of ultimism makes sense and is true. No doubt there may be many things about an ultimate person that we couldn't understand; its way of being a person may be very different from our own. But it would be odd to shrink from the implications of what we do understand about persons—for example, what it is for persons to love other persons—when our aim is given *by inquiry*: to determine whether personal ultimism is true. If there actually being a loving personal ultimate seems strongly to have implications that are not realized in the world, then it would be better, certainly from the standpoint of investigation, to set aside the personal interpretation of ultimism and move on to some other.

Now perhaps some critics will be inclined to resist the main premise of the hiddenness argument because of a prior commitment to a religious scripture or creed incompatible with it or in tension with it. Isn't the God of the Bible, for example, often portrayed as somewhat distant relationally? But I suspect you'll be able to see how such a move falls short. Notice, first of all, that its source is loyalty to preconceived views instead of a burning desire to know what's true here, no matter what that may be. The reason for resistance is not investigation-based. Second, and more important, the pictures of the Bible are framed by people *with the same sort of loyalty*, who assume that a person-like God actually exists and are trying to understand and submit to "his" ways. It's not surprising that religious conceptions from the Bible are so often in sync with facts in the world that trouble philosophers, when they were designed to be so!

A more sensitive and appropriate suggestion here might be that, whatever their source or motivation, biblical or creedal depictions of God *could contain insights,* and we should look to see whether they do. I agree. We should. But the vital question is this. Can we find in these depictions insights about relational matters, including the impulses of love, that run counter to the hiddenness argument's main premise? What one finds is a good bit of patriarchal material, with God depicted as a King or Father, whose loving behavior alternates with wrathful displays. I don't see a convincing or insightful depiction of the greatest possible person in this material. And material that's more impressive, even against the background of all that we humans have learned about social and gender relations and about the immaturity of violence, actually *supports* the hiddenness argument's main premise, coming out strongly in favor of sharing and giving and reliable openness—consider, for example, the relevant teachings of Jesus of Nazareth.

I suggest, therefore, that one is grasping at straws if one seeks on such grounds as those mentioned here to resist the main premise of the hiddenness argument.

CHAPTER 5

ADD INSIGHT AND STIR

When I was studying at Oxford in the late '80s of the last century, my overriding aim was to develop the argument that most fully and forcefully gave voice to the neglected considerations set out in Chapter 3 of this book. Now don't misunderstand. It's not as though I was already convinced by it, before I had even knocked it into shape. In fact, I would have been quite willing to discover that the strongest argument of the relevant sort was still not strong enough. In that case I would have developed the second part of *Divine Hiddenness and Human Reason* rather differently. But respect for the truth requires that before one adopts such mega-opinions as the opinion that there is a God, one must consider the arguments that most powerfully test them. And I sensed that the hiddenness argument, not yet fully born, was one of the arguments we needed to be aware of to carry out the relevant tests with proper thoroughness. I also sensed that, in developing the argument, it would be good to start "from above" with facts about the concept of God—in particular a loving God.

Though I didn't then make conspicuous use of the notion of openness that figured so prominently in Chapter 4, what I had come up with by the fall of 1988 and felt I could defend to just about anyone was in fact logically equivalent to the premise that emerges unscathed from our discussion there. Here it is again:

If a perfectly loving God exists, then there exists a God who is always open to a personal relationship with any finite person.

What we have here, as you'll recall, is an If/then or conditional proposition. The second part (the bit coming after "then") logicians will call the *consequent* of that proposition. This consequent taken by itself, makes the crucial statement about openness:

There exists a God who is always open to a personal relationship with any finite person.

In the last chapter we saw how the content of this statement, as defined there, conceptually "comes along with" the first part of our main premise—what logicians will call its *antecedent*:

A perfectly loving God exists.

Where this proposition about perfect love is true, the proposition about openness will be true too. In the present chapter I want to show how, with just a touch of insight, we can take things an important step further, noticing that the consequent of our main premise can become the antecedent for a new conditional proposition—and new premise—that has the following shape:

If there exists a God who is always open to a personal relationship with any finite person, then no finite person is ever nonresistantly in a state of nonbelief in relation to the proposition that God exists.

As you can see, the information added in the consequent of this new premise is the following:

No finite person is ever nonresistantly in a state of nonbelief in relation to the proposition that God exists.

Take a first good look at the whole premise to see whether you find it at least initially plausible to suppose that the truth of this additional information would come along with God's openness to personal relationship, just as such openness comes along with perfect love.

The basic idea here, as you may have observed, is that participating in a meaningful conscious relationship with God is bound up with *believing* in God. This is the fundamental insight my chapter title refers to, and by stirring it a bit we'll generate, in this chapter, the first conclusion drawn by the hiddenness argument.

Resistance

But before doing that, let's say a little more about the notions of *resistance* and *nonresistance,* which we need to understand to assess our new premise. We saw in the previous chapter that openness to relationship with finite persons, on God's part, is being treated by the hiddenness argument as consistent with God letting creatures shut the door to relationship themselves. For it's widely held that if God creates finite persons God will give them free will. Indeed, this too some would connect to divine love, which they regard as necessarily letting things be what they want to be. And such free will, most theists and also many non-theists will say, could hardly be respected by God if God prevented creatures from freely putting *themselves* in a position where they could no longer notice God's overtures or participate in relationship with God just by trying to.

It's because I'm going along with these assumptions for the sake of this discussion that resistance comes up at all. If we didn't include this qualification, our new premise would say, more simply, that a God open to relationship would ensure that everyone always believed no matter what. And this would run contrary to what a sensitivity to the importance of free will requires, since one way in which creatures might freely behave, so it will be said, involves *resistantly deceiving themselves on whether there is a God, and falling into doubt or disbelief about this matter as a result.*

When I first developed the hiddenness argument I was inclined to speak of these things in terms of culpability and inculpability rather than in terms of resistance and nonresistance, as I do today. What I had in mind was that given God's loving openness to relationship, no finite creature would ever fail to believe in God *without it being their own fault.* I was in fact thinking about resistance of God but I thought that such resistance, which would have to come in the face of evidence of a good and loving Maker to whom one owed everything, would clearly be blameworthy. And I developed my reasoning within the context created by this thought, arguing that there would be no non-blameworthy or inculpable nonbelief if there were a loving God and then also—later in the argument—that such nonbelief does in fact exist.

I now see this focus on culpability and inculpability as a mistake. Nonbelief might conceivably be culpable in many ways, and by making these moves at the beginning of the argument I was forcing it ultimately to support the view that there is, in the actual world, nonbelief that in *none* of these ways is owed to culpable behavior. I wanted the best developed and most forceful hiddenness argument, but this was not the way to get it.

So for some time now I have been sticking to the narrower focus on resistance. If we truly start "from above," thinking first about love and then about openness and then about what it would take for God to allow someone *not* to be in a position to participate in a personal relationship with the divine, we will see that a sort of free resistance sufficient to make it the case that we ourselves have shut the door to any relationship with God that might be on offer would be required. To trade one metaphor for another, if God is open to personal relationship then the divine light will remain on unless we close our eyes. The self-deceptive resistance required would include a desire component: a desire not to be in a relationship with God, or else to be in a condition incompatible with relationship with God. We might imagine a resister wanting to do her own thing without considering God's view on the matter, or wanting to do something she regards as in fact contrary to the values cultivated in a relationship with God. But it would also involve *actions or omissions* (at least mental ones) in support of such desire—actions or omissions which have the result that, self-deceived, one no longer believes in the existence of God, although one did to begin with. Here we might imagine careless investigation of one sort or another in relation to the existence of God, or someone deliberately consorting with people who carelessly fail to believe in God and avoiding those who believe, or just over time mentally drifting, with her own acquiescence, away from any place where she could convincingly be met by evidence of God.

I want to underline here that what our new premise is saying with the words "no finite person is ever nonresistantly in a state of nonbelief..." is not simply that any person who is in a state of nonbelief *is also resistant*, perhaps in a manner causally unrelated to her nonbelief. It says that any finite person who is in a state of nonbelief is so *because* of resistance. The causal tie between resistance and nonbelief in a world including a loving God needs to be remembered. For without resistance causing nonbelief, a loving God's openness to relationship would be such as to ensure that belief in God was never lost.

Belief

But *why* must this be the case? It's time to look at this more closely. One quick way of doing so involves noticing the plausibility of a certain general principle about openness and non-openness. I call it *Not Open* because it identifies a condition in which, at a certain time, a person B clearly is not open to relationship with a second person A.

Let's work up to the principle with a thought experiment. Suppose that you've been adopted and you're wondering whether your biological mother is still out there somewhere. You don't believe she is but you don't resist the idea. It's certainly not the case that you're in that state of nonbelief about her *due* to your resistance of the idea. (We could imagine someone in your situation being told by a reliable source that his biological mother is in town and blotting out the thought because he just doesn't want to see her. But your condition isn't anything like that.) Now suppose also that your biological mother *is* in the area, and that she has been told that you wonder about her but don't know what to believe on the matter of whether she's still alive. She's in a position to let you know that she's there, but doesn't do so. Here's the question: Is your biological mother open to having, *at that time*, a personal, interactive relationship with you? Just as we saw in the previous chapter, in connection with a somewhat similar example, the answer is clearly no. Let's generalize from this example and produce our principle:

Not Open
If a person A, without having brought about this condition through resistance of personal relationship with person B, is at some time in a state of *nonbelief* in relation to the proposition that B exists, where B at that time knows this and could ensure that A's nonbelief is at that time changed to belief, then it is not the case that B is open at the time in question to having a personal relationship with A then.

Think about it. Here's A, who isn't even aware that B exists (and without having put himself into that condition). B knows this and *could* reveal herself but chooses not to. In these circumstances, how could it still be the case that B is open to a meaningful, conscious relationship with A then? After all, by not revealing herself B is doing something that makes it impossible for such a relationship to exist at that time, and this, according to our definition, is precisely what is involved in not then being open to it.

We can apply this to God, who of course possesses *all* relevant knowledge and ability: if some finite person is ever nonresistantly in a state of nonbelief in relation to God's existence, then there is no God who is *always* open to a personal relationship with any finite person. Another way of putting that point, approved by logic, gives us our new premise: if there exists a God who is always open to a personal relationship with each finite person, then no finite person is ever nonresistantly in a state of nonbelief in relation to the proposition that God exists.

Now this reasoning has a lot of intuitive force. But for it to work we need two conditions to be in place: (1) it has to be the case that believing in the existence of the other person, in this case God, is necessary to participate in a conscious, interactive, and positively meaningful relationship with her (which, recall, is the full articulation of "personal relationship" as I am using that term), and (2) it also has to be the case that we can't come up with such belief on our own, just by trying to. It's pretty clear that these conditions *are* in place, but in a responsible discussion we need to spend at least a bit of time on why this is true. So let's do that now.

Think first about what it would be to participate in such a meaningful, conscious relationship with God. Notice, as you think about this, that we don't have to conceive of such a relationship in the "chummy" way that, say, a certain sort of contemporary Christian might. "Conscious, interactive, and positively meaningful relationship" is compatible with a whole lot of quite different detailed descriptions, including ones according to which the proper response to God is one of humble gratitude or a rigorous search for insight into God's will for one's life and difficult work in carrying it out. And God's proper response to *us* might be described not in terms of continually warm and fuzzy religious experiences that fail to challenge us but rather with reference to something like discernible assistance in the slow shaping of a finite and perhaps recalcitrant personality, through the offering of such things as forgiveness and emotional support. The common content of all such descriptions, though, is a pattern of *reciprocal* activity directed toward ever deeper and richer interaction in which both God and finite creatures participate and which both find valuable.

Now ask yourself: how can anyone express gratitude for what she has experienced as a gift of God's grace or try to find God's will for her life or recognize God's forgiveness or do or experience any of the hundred similar things involved in a conscious, reciprocal relationship with God *if she does not believe that God exists?* It's impossible. To be grateful to someone in the manner of conscious relationship, you have to believe they exist. Ditto for trying to figure out what they favor or recognizing that they've forgiven you or are offering you moral support and their encouraging presence.

Perhaps someone will still be inclined to resist by saying that *hope* or even a certain kind of beliefless *faith* could replace belief, at least at the start of a meaningful conscious relationship with God. If subsequently belief arose, and at the end of her life the person in question were to be asked when she thinks her personal relationship with God began, would she be *mistaken* if she were to pick the time when her hope or faith began, rather than the time when she came to believe?

Well, if she uses the phrase "personal relationship" in the same way we are using it she would be—a conscious relationship is one you recognize yourself to be in as opposed to hoping you're in. (One can't solve the hiddenness problem just by noting that the terms it employs and to which it gives certain senses can be used in different senses.) But to get at the deeper issue here: when belief comes to someone who had thought there might be no God, the change of her perceived relation to God is a change not just in degree but in *kind*. It is much different than, say, a move from hoping with intensity x that God exists to hoping this with intensity x + 1 or even x + 10. Indeed, in a very real sense now *everything* has changed for her, for what she hoped has (as she sees it) come true! And it is in part because of this difference for the one she loves that the one who loves him will naturally want this to be where things *start* in the story of their interaction. So from both perspectives, the perspective of the lover and that of the one loved, the relationship made possible by belief is a different relationship than any left to subsist on hope or nonbelieving faith.

Consider now the second condition that, as mentioned above, needs to be in place if the previous reasoning is to be effective. Is it really true that we can't believe in the existence of God just by trying to? If we *could* do so, God might be open to personal relationship with us while expecting us to produce this prerequisite for it on our own.

But a bit of reflection will close the door to this thought. Whatever may be true of other attitudes such as assuming or accepting a proposition for the sake of discussion, you can't change or add to your *beliefs* just by trying to. Experiment with this a little if you're not convinced. You'll see that believing isn't that sort of psychological condition; in fact, believing is *involuntary*. If it weren't, we'd have a quick cure for all sorts of problems. Feeling depressed? Just believe you're on top of the world! Worried about being overweight? Just believe you're not! Unsure about the existence of God, Pascal? Well, don't you know that you can believe that God exists in the same way you can raise your arm into the air, just by trying to?

The genius Pascal would try to tamp down your enthusiasm—even though he's often construed as arguing that *over time* you can do things that have the effect of producing a belief initially thought to be poorly evidenced. (What he couldn't do is show that if your aim was belief, this wouldn't be dishonest and so still a strategem unlikely to be favored by a perfectly good God.) You can't produce beliefs at the drop of a hat, just by trying to. But if you can't produce beliefs at the drop of a hat, and if conscious relationship and belief really do go together, then when you don't believe that God exists, you're not in a position *then* to participate in relationship with God just by trying to. And this gives the green light to our principle from before, *Not Open*. To put it in terms we used in Chapter 4, a loving God's openness to meaningful, conscious relationship with us means that such a God will ensure that we always *are* in a position to participate in it—unless of course we've disqualified *ourselves* through self-deceptive resistance toward God. It follows that in the absence of such resistance, a loving God will ensure that you always believe that God exists. Putting this just a bit more fully and formally yields, again, our new premise:

> If there exists a God who is always open to a personal relationship with any finite person, then no finite person is ever nonresistantly in a state of nonbelief in relation to the proposition that God exists.

Goods

Seeing that openness to relationship on the part of a loving God is enough to make for the prevention of nonresistant nonbelief, and smelling, intellectually, that this may lead to problems, those who oppose the argument may now be inclined to resist the idea that God *would be* thus open—which is, in effect, to go back to the argument's main premise and say "Hey, I know I bought this, but now I'm not so sure!" Despite appearances, this needn't be an intellectually dishonest move, but to avoid the latter criticism new reasons for reticence about our main premise will be needed. And after seeing what openness implies in relation to a loving God's facilitation of *belief*, it would be natural for these to be reasons for supposing that even a loving God needn't do *that*. Adjusting this slightly: we might hope to find reasons for supposing that even a loving God would or might at some time allow nonresistant nonbelief (which, as the reasoning of this chapter has shown, God could do only by sacrificing openness at that time).

The reasons that have been or may be put forward will tend to focus on certain *good* things that seem to require that nonresistant nonbelief be permitted and thus might tempt a perfectly loving God to permit it, even at the cost of openness. I hope you'll remember, as we discuss them, the more abstract points from Chapter 4 about how we might expect any goods the critic cares to mention—or reasonable facsimiles thereof—to be ones that can be encountered precisely *through* a relationship with an infinitely rich divine reality. Indeed, I'll be helping you to do so. For in discussing these more meaty reasons for God to allow nonresistant nonbelief, we'll have a chance to put some flesh on those conceptual bones.

So what are the relevant goods? Let's look at some that are representative of those that have lately been mentioned in journal articles and books.

(i) *Avoidance of a negative response to God that harms the future prospects of the relationship*. The idea here is that some nonresistant nonbelievers who haven't ever believed might be in this condition because, through no fault of their own, they are disposed in such a way that, had belief in God been made available to them, they would very likely have responded by *rejecting* God. (For example, it may be thought that there are immature but nonresistant nonbelievers who would likely have become resentful over evils they or their loved ones have been made to suffer, and blamed God, had they at an earlier time been converted to belief.) Might not a loving God, who wants a positively meaningful relationship, seek to *avoid* this and therefore prevent the belief of such individuals?

This may sound like a plausible bit of reasoning, but we should wonder why an unsurpassably great person would have no way to either avoid or transform such a negative response short of hiding. Imagine ideally loving human parents-to-be who are aware, because of their knowledge of the unborn child's genetic constitution, that this child will be disposed to reject them. (Notice that we cannot say he is certain to do so and powerless to do otherwise or we will no longer have a relevant analogy: given how the hiddenness argument is set out, the nonbeliever, and so this child, have to be and remain *capable* of a more positive relationship.) Will they exit stage left, once the baby is born, leaving it in the care of someone they think is more likely to elicit a positive response, or rather seek to devise ways of avoiding or transforming their child's negative response from *within* their relationship with him?

The second option seems clearly correct. And when we adjust for the differences between human beings and God, we find more rather than less reason to say the same thing about God: to say that God would work from *within* the circumstances of intellectual closeness to the nonbeliever to deal with such problems rather than—by preventing belief in God—taking the radical step of not producing such circumstances in the first place. Pascal, despite thinking God would hide, helps to show this by suggesting what a non-hidden God could do through religious experience to address any number of responses in the context of a continuing conscious relationship (he uses Christian language but his point can be applied more broadly): "The God of the Christians is a God of love and consolation: he is a God who fills the soul and heart of those whom he possesses: he is a God who makes them inwardly aware of their wretchedness and his infinite mercy: who unites himself with them in the depths of their soul: who fills it with humility, joy, confidence, and love: who makes them incapable of having any other end than him."

Pascal's idea, adapted for the occasion, is that a loving God rebuffed in anger (assuming for the sake of discussion that such a thing might occur) would regard this as just one move in a complex reciprocal relationship unfolding over much time, and work to promote a more mature response *in the context of the relationship* in the way loving people do. Human beings, of course, can be present to each other physically, but even if this is impossible in the case of God, God could still be present to us experientially in an amazing range of ways, communicating with us, as it were, from within. Such faithfulness to the relationship would have great *intrinsic value*—value in itself, quite apart from any value it might have as a means to an end. But even if we were thinking purely about the effectiveness of such a reaction on God's part (about what philosophers would call its *instrumental* value, its value as a means to an end), wouldn't we have to conclude that continued openness, appropriately implemented to meet the occasion, would be more likely to facilitate the growth of a meaningful and positive relationship over time than a retreat into hiddenness involving the absence of belief? Notice, for example, how misleading such hiddenness would be: it would lead the nonresistant creature into legitimate doubt as to whether God even exists, giving her that much more to complain about when God *does* come on the scene. In short, God's *attempt to experientially transform* a negative response in the context of a continuing relationship would have much more value than just its avoidance by means of hiddenness—and might indeed be expected to contribute to the prevention of similar responses in the future.

One may find it strange that responses to the hiddenness argument such as the "avoidance" response we are considering here even suggest themselves to people who have thought about what an unsurpassably great and loving person would be able to do. But we may be able to understand this if we notice that objections of this sort are often produced by people operating within what is essentially a theological context—people who believe in God and who are trying to explain what they regard as a literal hiddenness of God. Such people may notice other people who really are "angry at God" in an ongoing way and—because they are assuming God exists—infer that *this sort of thing really can happen even when God exists,* and that it can help to explain hiddenness. Especially when those who might respond resentfully (or otherwise negatively) are young and immature, so it may be said, God might well want to give them some time to grow up before becoming known to them, to make a positive response to God's self-revelation more likely. Indeed, this way of thinking can come to seem quite plausible to someone who believes that God exists.

But considering the hiddenness argument appropriately, as an argument *against* the existence of God, means putting oneself into a very different frame of mind, at least for the sake of discussion. One has to drop the assumption that God exists and that everything somehow fits God's plan (atheism can't even be taken seriously if *that's* one's frame of mind!), mentally bringing together the two relevant concepts: the concept of a finite person at least initially disposed to respond negatively to God, and that of a creator of all, a Person unlimitedly wonderful and resourceful. And one has to think about what a person of the latter kind could do for one of the former kind—*without regard to what is in fact available to believers and nonbelievers in the actual world and without the assumption that this indicates what God could or would do.* Such thinking may of course be difficult for someone who believes in God and indeed for anyone who lives in a culture saturated with theistic belief, but it's exactly what's required to assess the hiddenness argument *philosophically,* as much as possible without bias. And it's therefore also necessary to discover what needs to be said about the various goods that are put forward as reasons for hiddenness. In that frame of mind, let's turn to the next such good.

(ii) *Genuine or deep freedom to choose one's own destiny, morally speaking.* The idea this time is that if God seems close to you instead of hidden and you therefore believe in God, you may find yourself with few desires to do bad things (temptations) of the sort that morally good people freely overcome, because it will so obviously be in your best interest not to do such actions (and this whether you think God would punish you for doing them or not, since a perfectly good being's approval can motivate too). This means that you will in fact lack the sort of freedom morally good people have and the opportunity to determine what sort of person you will be, good or bad. Or at least some especially impressionable or sensitive people may lack this valuable sort of freedom unless they are prevented from believing in God. The upshot? We shouldn't expect God to get rid of or prevent *all* nonresistant nonbelief.

This "free will" defence against the hiddenness argument may at first sight appear inconsistent with the previous defence, which imagined God trying to *avoid* a certain free response on the part of finite persons. And indeed it may seem to suggest something plausible I could have added when considering that defence: since free will is so important, wouldn't God want to allow the *free negative response of believers*? Back to the apparent inconsistency: if finite persons are even *able* to respond negatively to God, doesn't this show they have plenty of freedom of the sort it is here said God can preserve only by hiding?

But there is also a way of resolving this difficulty which we'll see when we notice that the previous defence may take itself to be talking about a particular *sort* of finite person and the free will defence may take itself to be talking about a very *different* sort. Some people, indeed, might be able to exercise free will even in the presence of God (so we should suppose our new defence to be saying)—maybe even by lashing out at God—but others whose will is more weak or morally sensitive are not able to do so, and from them God may hide.

Having developed this free will move as charitably as we can (as is appropriate in a philosophical discussion aimed at the truth, whatever that may turn out to be), what should we say about it? Does it defeat the hiddenness argument's main premise by showing that something it implies—that God would make uninterrupted belief in God available for everyone in the absence of resistance—is or might be false?

I don't think so. Even if free will helps with the problem of evil, it doesn't help *here*, with this different problem. Notice first that just to get started, this move has to assume that God would or might create people like those we find in the actual world, including morally weak and impressionable ones. But why should we suppose that? Isn't this the same problem we saw under (i) above—the tendency to focus on what we find in the actual world because, so it's illegitimately assumed, *that's* the world God must have created if indeed God exists? Why should we suppose that a God would create us, or people like us? Why mightn't God create very different people, if God creates people at all? A philosopher has to be open on this even if a theologian doesn't.

Perhaps the answer will be that even philosophers can't rule out the idea that God *might* create people of the relevant sort, maybe by permitting them to come into existence through some evolutionary process. This answer shouldn't be convincing. Why would a loving God permit the unfolding of an evolutionary process that stymied some of the aims of love, especially when there are other ways things could have been made to go, compatible with both loving openness and a free and responsible choice of destiny for finite created persons?

But let's relinquish this point in order to focus on a deeper one: that even if there are people of the relevant sort in the world God creates, hiddenness is in no way necessary for them to have the goods that we are discussing, associated with free will. The alternative view assumes that God would seem close to us, present to our experience, if the hiddenness argument is right—always there and noticeably so. But all the hiddenness argument claims is that those who are nonresistant will believe: it doesn't say that this will be the case because God is present to their experience—and it certainly doesn't say or even suggest that God would constantly or overwhelmingly or intrusively be present to anyone's experience. Anyone who thinks such things is influenced by a caricature of the argument, not the real thing.

There are in fact various ways in which nonresistant people might legitimately become—and stay—believers in God in a world in which God really exists and is inclined to have them be believers. Evidence of events from around the world that seem to everyone who nonresistantly considers them to be, on balance, best explained by the activity of God could be made universally available. This would not be psychologically intrusive even when effective in producing and maintaining belief in God. Or everyone everywhere could be gifted with a continuing quiet sense of God's existence on par with belief in other minds or belief in an external world—and I mean a sense of *God*, with the concept of a loving and ultimate Person clear in everyone's mind, not what passes for it in some quarters of the actual world. This wouldn't need to be intrusive or constantly in the forefront of one's awareness any more than is the belief in God of people today in regions or households (like my own growing up) where the existence of God is just taken for granted, along with the existence of trees and horses and people. Belief could of course also be produced through a more direct experience of God. One can imagine, for example, a powerful initial experience of God's presence that everyone has followed by a lingering background awareness. And of course religious experience is the sort of thing that could be *modulated* by God to fit people's circumstances as they changed, in ways we have seen suggested by Pascal. This means that for those who are especially sensitive or vulnerable to moral influence, the sense of God's presence could recede or even be withdrawn altogether in moments of temptation. The possibilities here are indeed limited only by the imagination.

There's another point that should briefly be made about free will, too. Maybe you've noticed how people who appeal to it in explanations of hiddenness assume that to have it you have to be able to do *morally bad* things. After all, it's your desire to do such things that we might expect to be affected by having God in the forefront of your awareness, because of self-interestedness. But is the assumption right? It seems not, since there are at least two ways in which you could still have a highly significant form of moral freedom even if you never desired to do anything bad.

First, you could work at changing the motive underlying your constant attempt to do good. Here you are (let's suppose) doing what is good because, sensitive to God's presence, you think it's in your interest to do so. But you also realize that a better motive is to do the good because, well, because it's *good*! So you have a chance to work at changing your motive or at least add a new one—and what's this if not a morally significant way of exercising free will?

Second, there are not only actions that are morally *right* (meaning obligatory) and others that are morally *wrong* (which we are obligated not to do). There are also actions that are—as we say—above and beyond the call of duty. Philosophers label such actions "morally supererogatory." Don't ask me why. There are indeed lots and lots of such actions—endless ways of doing *more* good than you are *required* to do by duty or obligation, and so of moving beyond those actions that God's presence (we are supposing) makes you want to do for the self-interested reason that it will avoid divine punishment or disapproval. So you remain morally free, and significantly so, in this way: you can choose whether to mold your life into one overflowing with such actions, or do what you have to do, morally speaking, and then slouch on the couch. What is this if not a choice of destiny?

In these ways we see once more how God can gain for us significant moral freedom while displaying openness to relationship too, and so lacks any reason to give up the latter for the former, even in the situation we have here (quite implausibly) been supposing would exist if the impressionable among us were to believe that there is a God.

(iii) *A chance to develop deep longing for God, which might help someone grow spiritually and so should be viewed as a good thing.* Having their belief in God become elusive or disappear, we are told, might be just the right thing to help some people who are nonresistant toward God go beyond such nonresistance to a deeper spirituality.

Thinking about the multi-layered nature of relationship with a personal Ultimate (and the desires that the perhaps just-out-of-reach depths of God would continually provoke), readers will probably be able to provide a response to this suggestion by themselves. A relationship with *God* would not be a flat one-dimensional thing that, once you have it, means all the interesting searching for God is over. Instead, in a very important sense a life of religious searching would just be beginning. Think, by analogy, of your relationship with a wise guru or even the tennis pro you, as an amateur, are consulting to improve your tennis. You're constantly learning and growing, but you also realize that there's so much more to be attained and this squeezes out of you even more interesting desires than you had at the beginning, desires for this or that subtle feature of wisdom or of excellence in tennis you can have only by proceeding beyond the beginning. These are of course only humble analogies. But their very humbleness is helpful when—as you knew I was going to ask you to do—you imagine by comparison being in a relationship with God, an *infinitely* interesting, rich, beautiful, sublime (etc. etc.) Person.

Here it's also worth remembering what the Spanish mystic, St. John of the Cross, called "the dark night of the soul"—an experience in which, though one believes in God, one endures mental suffering and a sense of God as darkness or as faraway light which is said to deepen and purify one's relation to God. Plenty of room for the development of a deep longing for God here! (The mystics, like Pascal, help to stretch our imagination—and this even if they should be in touch with no divine reality, or at least with no personal divine reality.) In fact, the idea of the dark night of the soul is more generally helpful too. For, as can be seen, it suggests a way in which God can be hidden even *within* relationship. What we have here is really a secondary sort of hiddenness quite compatible with belief in God. One may wonder whether it's similar enough to the primary sort of hiddenness. But the only similarity needed is that the secondary sort of hiddenness be able to pave the way for at least some of the goods that are said to require that someone *not* believe in God—such as the good of a deep longing for God. And this can be seen to be the case.

(iv) *The opportunity to exhibit a noble sort of courage or love that sacrifices itself for the good even where no belief in a happy afterlife exists to diminish its value.* The idea here is that belief in a loving God brings with it belief in a happy afterlife, which stands in the way of certain specific moral goods that God might well wish some of us to have the opportunity to experience.

This argument I find more interesting than many of the others. But it too is fairly easily answered when we use our imagination to think about a relationship with God properly. Immediately we can see that the dark night of the soul is again relevant: would belief in a happy afterlife really cut through the darkness sufficiently to prevent courage from being required to deal with it? But, so you say, the courage that is referred to by the answer to the hiddenness argument we're considering may be the wonderful courage involved in *laying down one's life for others.* One response is that courage is courage: what makes courage valuable in the latter case is present in the former too. But let's look specifically at laying down one's life for others. Must belief in a happy afterlife really enter into such noble sacrifices (for those who hold that belief) or really make such sacrifices easier, if God implants or allows to be implanted in persons a strong urge toward self-preservation? And why, anyway, must the expected afterlife be "happy" in a manner immediately effective given self-protective desires instead of morally demanding—requiring a courage all its own as one is invited to plunge ever deeper into an endless relationship with God?

(v) *The possibility of cooperative investigation into God's existence.* Finally, we have the idea that investigations into God's existence might be undertaken cooperatively by finite persons who nonresistantly fail to believe, and that this is a good thing.

Again we have the problem that what comes after belief in God and (perhaps) entry into relationship with God is being regarded somewhat unimaginatively, and so a brief reply will suffice. An endless stream of *deeper* investigations into the nature and will of God and into the nature of the world God has created might be undertaken cooperatively—perhaps with much more zest!—by nonresistant *believers.* And if this is so, we should not expect that a loving God would ever fail to be open to relationship for the sake of cooperative religious investigation.

Several general themes have emerged in my replies to these five reasons for God to allow nonresistant nonbelief. (1) The reasons offered are sometimes going to seem much more plausible in the context of some form of theology than in philosophy. (2) There are ways in which, given the infinite richness and depth of any loving God there may be, various goods can be accommodated *within* explicit relationship with God—which would itself be capable of an indefinite degree of development, with always more to discover and overcome for those who participated in it. What points like those we've examined provide us with reason to suppose God would value are often broad types of things—such as courage—that can be instanced (philosophers say "tokened") in various ways, and also in a developing relationship with God. If this is so, and if there is so *much* room for development in a real relationship with God, why should such relationship ever be postponed or interrupted for the sake of those goods? (3) We've also seen a way of deepening this sort of response, one that apparently enables the hiddenness arguer to deal even with goods from the list that most seem to require the absence of belief in God's existence. This returns us to the literal meaning of "divine hiddenness," reminding us that there is a kind of divine withdrawal that can occur *within* relationship with God—producing a "dark night of the soul" *after* belief. The latter, because of its similar psychological effects, can readily substitute for a doubt inconsistent with belief in the production of relevant goods—and without misleading the nonbeliever on religious matters or removing the possibility of spiritually significant choices that strengthen the relationship.

Conclusion

In the conclusion to this chapter I want to show how given our main premise about openness, thus freshly defended, and the new premise about belief obviously connected to it, we can draw the hiddenness argument's first conclusion. This is a good time to remind you that interesting philosophical arguments often have more than one conclusion—they are chains of reasoning, with interim conclusions becoming premises to aid further reasoning until a *final* conclusion is drawn. That's what's going to happen in the hiddenness argument. From the two premises we have now discussed and seen to be solid results we will draw a conclusion. And then later, after adding a further premise, we'll use that conclusion together with the further premise to yield a new conclusion. The process will be repeated once after that too, as the dance of logic continues.

But that's in the future. For now, let's notice a particular way in which bits of reasoning can make a chain, with two If/then or conditional propositions taking us to a third on the iron rails of deduction. You'll recall that If/then propositions are really *two* propositions stuck together with the "if" and the "then" (it's that sticking together that makes them one.) Those two, as noted earlier, are called the antecedent and the consequent of the conditional. In logic you learn how to symbolize various relationships including those involved here. Contrary to what one may initially believe, logic does help us to see things more clearly! As evidence, let me symbolize the two conditional premises we have for the hiddenness argument so far. Just as in the Chapter 1 logic lesson, we'll use three variables—P, Q, and R—to stand, respectively, for the antecedent and consequent of the main premise and for the consequent of the new premise:

If P then Q.
If Q then R.

These are the logical skeletons of our two premises so far, discussed in this chapter and in Chapter 4. And here again are the premises themselves. Make sure you understand what we've done in symbolizing them before moving on (for added clarity I've marked the antecedent and consequent in each case with square brackets):

If [a perfectly loving God exists], then [there exists a God who is always open to a personal relationship with any finite person].

If [there exists a God who is always open to a personal relationship with any finite person], then [no finite person is ever nonresistantly in a state of nonbelief in relation to the proposition that God exists].

Do you see why we needed no fourth variable, S, to symbolize the antecedent of our second premise? It's because the antecedent of our second premise is the same as the consequent in the first premise. Precisely in this way our premises are interlocked, starting a chain.

The critical next step is to see how a third conditional proposition *follows* from our first two. Let's start again with symbols:

(1) If P then Q.
(2) If Q then R.
(3) If P then R (from 1 and 2).

This reasoning says that if a first thing leads to a second thing, and that second thing leads to a *third*, then the *first* leads to the third. The third conditional proposition *has* to be true if the first two are, and that's why it follows from them or makes a conclusion that can be drawn from them.

So if we apply this logic to our two premises, what do we get as a conclusion? Here are the three propositions; the third (in bold) is our conclusion:

If [a perfectly loving God exists], then [there exists a God who is always open to a personal relationship with any finite person].

If [there exists a God who is always open to a personal relationship with any finite person], then [no finite person is ever nonresistantly in a state of nonbelief in relation to the proposition that God exists].

If [a perfectly loving God exists], then [no finite person is ever nonresistantly in a state of nonbelief in relation to the proposition that God exists].

What do you suppose will be the next stop in this tour of the hiddenness argument?

CHAPTER 6

NONRESISTANT NONBELIEF

If you guessed that the next stop (or step) would involve considering whether any finite persons *have* nonresistantly failed to believe that God exists, then you were right—and then you're probably getting the hang of the hiddenness argument's reasoning to boot. But I add a cautionary note: we need to be getting the hang of *hiddenness* reasoning, not just of any reasoning with the progression of moves seen here. And that means respecting the approach "from above" and taking care to see exactly what it is we're saying when we say, as the argument in its next premise now does, that nonresistant nonbelief exists:

> Some finite persons are or have been nonresistantly in a state of nonbelief in relation to the proposition that God exists.

If I had started "from below" when developing the hiddenness argument, I might have focused, when thinking about nonresistant nonbelief, on my own religious doubt and that of others like me and the wrenching difficulties—emotionally, socially, and in other ways—that often come with it. I might have developed thoughts of the sort that, in Chapter 3, we found in Nietzsche, Hepburn, and Schlesinger and produced a version of the problem of evil that fizzled out when it met the broad answers theists have for centuries been offering to questions about suffering and the seeming injustice of God. But instead approaching the matter "from above," thinking about divine love in a different way than you'll find in any discussion of the problem of evil, what we've learned is that the troublesome phenomenon is indeed to be identified as *nonresistant nonbelief*. To put it somewhat inelegantly:

what the machine of our reasoning has spit out is a much broader category than any sort of doubt. Anguished doubt may provide an *example* of nonresistant nonbelief, but it's not the same thing. Even if there had never been any anguished doubt, there might still be non-resistant nonbelief. Nor is the relevant notion of nonbelief to be identified with any sort of *dis*belief—believing that there is no God. A certain kind of disbelief in God, that is, nonresistant atheism, just like a certain kind of doubt, provides an example of nonresistant nonbelief, but no more than that. To speak of "nonbelief" in this context is to speak simply of *not believing in God*—and such "not believing" can appear in many different ways.

Why is this important? Because it's relevant to any defence of the sort I'm now going to give of the claim that the troublesome phenomenon identified by the hiddenness argument *actually exists*. Having pinpointed the problem for theism, we need to go looking to see whether nonresistant nonbelief appears in the world. And there are many more ways of finding it than one might initially think. Influenced by other approaches, we might think it has to be this or that specifically—maybe a case of reflective *doubt* that is blameless in every way—when in fact that's not required. Indeed, some writers responding to the hiddenness argument have proceeded in just this manner, thinking they could defeat the argument if they could show that cases of nonbelief like my own past doubt might not be entirely blameless. But these efforts don't come close to succeeding because they're too narrowly focused.

I have to admit that I'm partially responsible for the irrelevant responses of such writers. In *Divine Hiddenness and Human Reason* I myself focused on reflective doubt—blamelessly caused. As I've noted, even if this isn't the same as nonresistant or inculpable nonbelief, it does provide an *example* of it; so if you can show it exists you've shown that nonresistant nonbelief exists. Some of my commentators still erred in thinking that proof of inculpable doubt was *necessary* for proof of inculpable nonbelief instead of just sufficient, but I made it easier for them to do so. Incidentally, my reason for focusing on doubt back then had little to do with my own doubt. Rather, I thought it might be more interesting for *investigators* to discuss *investigative* doubt. I also thought this sort of inculpable nonbelief might be harder to prove than others, and nobly decided to do the hard thing rather than the easy one.

But I've long since given up on nobility, so here I plan to start with the easy case.

Pre-Doubt

If the universe and planet Earth had—as was long believed—come into being a few thousand years ago, say, at around the time when people in the Ancient Near East began talking about a loving creator of all things, life would be a lot easier for many members of the theistic religions. Jewish, Christian, and Islamic intellectuals would have fewer headaches. Or if intelligent and spiritually sensitive beings, beings with the basic capacities required for relationship with God, had evolved suddenly just a few thousand years ago, we'd have the same result.

As it is, the most powerful and strikingly successful tools those intelligent beings have yet crafted—the methods of science—make it impossible for any serious investigator to doubt that the universe and our planet have been around for a lot longer than that. And when I say a lot, I mean A LOT. Among science's discoveries is the discovery of deep time: the universe is not thousands or even millions but many *billions* of years old, and its possible future can't be described without using the same vertigo-inducing numbers. We might not have guessed this without science since our own daily comings and goings are governed by human timescales measuring time in hours and days and years, but there it is. The past life of our planet too has to be measured in billions of years, and for most of this time life has been creeping through multiple avenues, with the evolutionary mechanism of natural selection—perhaps among other factors—giving rise to innumerable creatures great and small. Creatures both wonderful and wise admittedly did not appear until relatively recently, but when a scientist considering these things says "relatively recently" she still has in mind periods a great deal longer than a few thousand years. The big-brained species of ape, *Homo sapiens*, emerged after (and alongside) other species already fairly well endowed in that department perhaps 200,000 years ago, and 50,000 years ago was using language and drawing pictures in caves and probably also engaging in religious or proto-religious behavior.

One reason why such a long prehistory for our species gives theists headaches is that it intensifies the problem of evil: nature has been even redder in tooth and claw than thinkers prior to Darwin knew, and for a lot longer. But another reason for headaches that is starting to make itself felt is that the theistic religions of Abraham, Jesus, and Muhammad come at the very end of a story of human religious or proto-religious activity much longer than their own, during a great deal of which God didn't explicitly figure at all, let alone as the main character. What hunter-gatherer societies before the invention of writing believed—or at any rate what *sort* of thing—is pieced together by scientists from many sources, including the practices of similar societies still found in remote parts of the world today. Gods and spirits of many kinds and many temperaments appear in such belief-structures, but a belief in just one God who has all power, all knowledge, is all good, and loves all people is conspicuous by its absence. And so in the lives of these hunter-gatherers and in their communities, stretching back many millennia before the dawn of recorded history and before anyone ever thought about "arguments for and against the existence of God," we find plenty of clear examples of *nonresistant nonbelief*.

Think about it. These are people who don't believe in God. So they are nonbelievers—they are not in a state of belief in relation to the proposition that God exists. And how could they be resistant? It's not even possible since resistance of God presupposes *thinking about* God, and their whole picture of the world is shaped in such a way that thinking about God just won't happen. It's not as though it couldn't happen. If a God had existed thirty thousand years ago and wanted to break through to some hunter-gatherer experientially, there'd have been nothing to stop it, since concepts with which the concept of God could have been formed in the moment of experience *were* possessed by such behaviorally modern humans: they had the basic concepts of power and wisdom; they knew what it was to love. So humans could have come to believe in God much earlier. Theistic religion didn't have to wait for tens of thousands of years more. But in at any rate many parts of the planet where *H. sapiens* and its thinking cousins roamed, it didn't happen. There's just too much evidence of God-exclusive thought forms among hunter-gatherers both then and now for it to be believed to be otherwise.

I say "in at any rate many parts of the planet" because I anticipate the objection that for all we know God *was* present to such individuals and groups without any information about their theism coming down to us. In fact every bit of evidence we have points the other way, but all the present defense of the hiddenness argument's premise about non-resistant nonbelief *needs* is that *some or many* prehistoric individuals or groups were such as to satisfy the description I have given, and this no serious investigator will dispute.

Another objection I anticipate says that the people I'm talking about did in a way believe in God, because they believed in one divine being higher than all others. But as Robert Wright shows with a nice survey of relevant scientific evidence in his book *The Evolution of God*, this was not the case in all hunter-gatherer societies, and where it was, the "high god," though "in some vague sense more important than other supernatural beings" and "often a creator god," was not a god "that controls the other gods." More important, the high god wasn't elevated in a *moral* sense; in hunter-gatherer societies, says Wright, the connection we are inclined to make between "god" and "good" is "just about unknown." Prehistoric high gods may have had a few of the characteristics God also has. But to say that because of this fact prehistoric humans were, through their interaction with the former, permitted a meaningful conscious relationship with the latter is like saying that by knowing Idi Amin, the brutal former president of

Uganda, I have come to know Nelson Mandela, because, after all, both were male, black, and president of an African country!

Doubt

So anyone with some acquaintance with evolutionary history and a willingness to look the truth in the eye will be able to see that, in the actual world, many people in our history have failed to believe in God without resistance of God in any way coming into the explanation of their nonbelief. Though somewhat self-centeredly we tend to focus on doubt or disbelief in our own time, perhaps the most obvious cases of nonresistant nonbelief occurred, as we might say, *pre-doubt*, persisting through many thousands of years in times long ago.

But having noted this, it's interesting to come back to the present and notice how the circumstances of today are hardly less damaging to the case of anyone who resists the idea of nonresistant nonbelief—though for different reasons. Even after thousands of years of theistic religion, and despite their knowledge of the best evidence theists have been able to advance for the existence of God, nonresistant nonbelievers remain among us. These are people who have looked at all the relevant evidence they could find—perhaps even lived it, in the case of experiential evidence—but who do not believe: that is, they are either in doubt about whether there is a God or they disbelieve. I'm going to focus on doubters, and on doubters who used to believe, but a very similar story could be told about many other reflective nonbelievers.

Let me say up front that there may also be *resistant* doubters and disbelievers, people whose condition of nonbelief is caused by the sorts of self-deceptive desires and behavior we discussed in connection with the concept of resistance in Chapter 5. Some believers would like to go further. It has proved tempting for some of those defending the existence of God against the hiddenness argument not only to assume that all candidate nonresistant nonbelievers must be alive today and in a state of explicit doubt or disbelief, but to suppose that the sorts of less salutary events that may for *some* of the latter produce nonbelief, as I've just conceded, may do so for *all*. As I'll now show, however, there is plenty of reason to think this view false. Believers should resist the temptation.

The basic reason is a simple one: in many cases of reflective doubt, it's precisely an *infusion of new information and reflection thereupon* that has caused it, not resistance of God. And continuing reflection causes the doubt to continue. Of course here a believer resisting the hiddenness argument, like a good prosecuting attorney, may wish to argue that it could be both: it could, in particular, be resistance of God that caused the sort of reflection that terminates in doubt! But pretend that you're a juror in the case rather than working for either the defence or the prosecution. What does the evidence show? What, in particular, is the context for the reflections of doubters that the prosecution is seeking to impugn?

By the time all the evidence has been laid out, what you will have heard is that the reflection of many doubters began while they were still believers, and quite happy and also quite busy in their belief. Sometimes the contrary information came out of the blue, unexpectedly: for example, in a university classroom where the happy believer was anticipating something quite different. They learned about the historical circumstances in which the scriptures on which they had always relied might have been formed, or for the first time studied the problem of evil, or had the difficulties in arguments for God expounded to them, or read about deep time, or encountered spiritual depth as well as religious experiences conflicting with their own in non-theistic religious traditions. Sometimes such people have pushed back at the apparent negative consequences of this new information for theistic belief (so that, ironically, what we have is resistance of the anti-God import of the evidence rather than resistance of God). People visited religious family members or friends or leaders at the local church or synagogue or mosque to get help with their questions, or read widely in religious literature, or fell on their knees in persistent prayer. But even so the doubt came. And belief involuntarily left. We've seen how belief is not directly subject to the will, so they were unable to stop the slide into doubt just by trying to. The best they could do was to research the God-question carefully and open their hearts, hoping that the path of evidence would in time turn the other way and religious equilibrium would be regained. But it didn't happen.

In broad outline, this story fits my own case. But I've heard many similar testimonies. And I want to emphasize that I don't intend to place any weight on my own case. You can pretend it's irrelevant. Someone who advances the hiddenness argument needn't be thinking about herself when she talks about nonresistant nonbelief: perhaps *other* nonbelievers strike her as displaying nonresistance by the same standards that leave her questioning her own. The broader point here is that as a juror in the case you get to listen not just to the doubters themselves but have available to you many other strands of evidence, such as testimony from people who knew those who now doubt and saw them struggling with it or who know of their honesty and love of the truth or who tell you they're sure the doubter would still love to be a believer. Facts are introduced into evidence about what the doubters were doing when they began to doubt and what they're doing now—facts which show many of them to be committed to causes at least as morally demanding as a religious commitment to God would be.

In response, you'll hear the believing prosecuters talk about how doubters *could* have been inattentive just when God was trying to get through. They *could* have been looking for a particular kind of evidence easy to manipulate or control, or pridefully demanding more evidence for God than they would look for in other contexts—perhaps because they want to have control over the direction of their lives instead of giving everything over to God. What people who say this sort of thing seize upon is the fact that human beings have many well advertised flaws and shortcomings. And what they will rhetorically ask is whether *any* of us can seriously claim that at no level (perhaps deep down) he or she is resisting the demands of a holy God.

As a juror in the case, however, you are required to take all such preaching with a grain of salt and keep your eye on the evidence—as well as on the precise question at issue, which is *not* whether the doubters on trial may have flaws, but on whether they may have been resisting God; and furthermore *not* whether resistance of one sort or another may be present, but whether there might be resistance of *the specific sort* that would remove belief in God—the sort of resistance that, as discussed in the previous chapter, amounts to closing one's eyes to the light of God, which would lead a loving God sadly to conclude that you don't want a relationship. Even if there are always going to be parts of one's character that fall short of perfection, and even if this means that all of us are at some level resistant to changes that would move us closer to what a God's character would be like, it in no way follows that when people stop believing in God, this sort of thing is always the explanation. And as the lives of many believers testify, it's possible to hang on to belief in God and preserve its comforts while through self-deception blunting or subverting the moral force of its implications. So we already know that resistance to God doesn't *always* lead to nonbelief. Indeed, someone who recognizes such moral facts about herself may at another level *appeal to God for help in making more of the needed changes*! Isn't this precisely what believers say we should do, and often see themselves as having done despite their imperfections? And mightn't someone who feels doubt growing in herself regret this fact precisely because she thereby loses such moral support—and for this very reason resist *the loss of belief* instead of resisting God?

So it would be a mistake to think, when people lose their belief in a perfect God, that it must be because all of us resist moral change in one way or another. Of course, if no direct evidence either way were available as to the condition of those who are reflectively in doubt about God's existence, this fact might lead someone reasonably to feel she could not rule out an explanation in terms of the relevant sort of resistance of God. But such evidence *is* available (all our juror has to do is open her ears to the many stories of doubt that present themselves to any inquiring mind), and because it is, and because much of it clearly points to nonresistance, we are in very different circumstances.

Given this support for the existence of nonresistant doubt, you, as a juror, would have to suspend all ordinary rules of testimony and evidence to conclude that there might not be any.

Secularity

In Chapter 3 I suggested that the deepening secularity of our culture contributes to our willingness these days to take the hiddenness argument seriously. And one way in which it does so is by making nonresistant doubt of the sort we've just been talking about more natural, less surprising—easier to accept as genuine. Cultural conditions after the short period in which theistic religion reigned are in many quarters becoming nearly as unfavorable to belief in the theist's God as the long periods that came before. Thus the fact of secularity helps hiddenness arguers to make their case when they reach the premise asserting the existence of nonresistant nonbelief.

Let me say a bit more about the "naturalness" of nonbelief in many parts of our culture, which is of central importance here. For people who spend all their time in the bosom of a deeply religious community, say, your typical small town with ten churches in the American Midwest or on the Manitoba prairie, religious nonbelief may seem deeply *un*natural. They and almost everyone they talk to—in the hall, on the street, in the post office, in restaurants—takes the existence of God for granted much as people take for granted that grass is green and that the sun rises in the east. Their life, in this respect, is similar to that of people in Europe 800 years ago, who lived in a time when pretty much every department of living was saturated with the assumption of God's existence.

And yet even *their* lives are profoundly different from the lives of the medievals in ways that have the fingerprints of secularity all over them. When they turn the dial on the radio they will hear almost exclusively nonreligious songs. Their newspapers will commonly have a "religion" page that is segregated from the rest of the paper. Driving down the road they obey laws whose justification, as everyone is at least dimly aware, derives from considerations that the nonreligious can accept as easily as the religious, and that are kept in place by secular authorities. And everyone knows that in "the city" life is very different, with religion even less (or differently) in evidence.

So let's go to the city. There are still churches here, though they are fewer and farther between. And they compete with synagogues and mosques and temples. Religion may be in the city too but it is pluralistic, and its pluralism will suggest to anyone growing up in the city or visiting it that there are many different ways of doing the religion thing. Think about that a bit longer and you may have the thought "Who knows which is right?" But then you may not think much about it at all, since diversity has become the new normal here.

Moreover religious institutions in the city, as in small towns, are clearly in various ways bowing their heads to secular authorities: they have to obey zoning laws and refrain from certain sorts of behavior within their sanctuaries just like everyone else everywhere else. Their capacity to "rule" is now restricted to the inner lives of their most devoted congregants. Even their schools, relatively few in number, will teach mostly material that is also taught in the much more numerous public schools, which are secular to a fault. If anything rules at school it's science, not religion.

Something similar is true of almost all institutions of *higher* learning—colleges and universities—in the city. The most estimable aspirations and attainments are thought, by people who spend time here, to be at least broadly scientific, and theology has long since been toppled from its position as the queen of the sciences. (Reflect on how ludicrous is the thought that it might regain that standing and you will see how far we've traveled into secularity.) People spend months and years and lifetimes in universities, as in many other spaces of the modern city, named and unnamed, without ever once thinking about God.

Even people in small religious towns tend to be aware that such things are true of life in the city and of the wider western world generally—which for most of them might as well be the whole world. Even for these people, then, who frown on it disapprovingly and deliberately shut themselves off from it, an utterly nonreligious way of life is *imaginable*. Nonbelief is not *entirely* unnatural. And for those who live it, it can be the most natural thing in the world, woven seamlessly into the larger fabric of life. Or, since we're talking about *non*belief, which can, as already suggested, be realized as a simple absence instead of an alternative presence, it has to be said that for many people the fabric of life is quite complete though it includes not a stitch of belief or its denial or even of doubt.

This "naturalness" of nonbelief has no parallel in the Middle Ages, when one could hardly have failed to believe in God without noticing it. It is in fact much more like the days of *pre*-doubt, except that then other and similar religious or proto-religious beliefs took the place of belief in God. Perhaps we should say that many in the modern world live *after* doubt, meaning not that they have doubted and moved on but, again, that their location in time is such that they can flourish without ever considering the question of God at all. I remember how surprised I was when, taking up my first summer job at an employment agency in the city of Calgary, Alberta, I discovered that the young man at the desk across from mine—an earnest and decent guy who I thought might be an evangelical Christian—had never thought about God at all. I was sure he was kidding. But he eventually convinced me. The subject had just never come up.

So what can the hiddenness arguer do with these facts? Certainly they don't by themselves prove there's no God: from the lone fact that people don't believe in God nothing follows as to whether there *is* a God! But they do aid in the support of the hiddenness argument's premise about nonresistant nonbelief. They help to show, to any religious person from the small town inclined to think that nonbelievers such as the doubter of our previous section must somehow be resisting God, that this need not be the case. When faced with clear evidence that this *isn't* the case, she will accordingly find the evidence harder to resist.

Believers who find that life brings them into the city may wonder why nonbelief has become natural there. Digging around a bit in university libraries or in the minds of friends from around the world or in the social media of cyberspace, they find information they would never have guessed was available while living in the small town—information that sharply conflicts with what they were taught to believe, that puts everything into a different perspective. And allowed in the city to think for themselves, to put their own minds to work on such information in ways they may have never had occasion to employ before, their former belief sometimes becomes just that: a thing of the past. Living on in reflective disbelief or doubt, they add their own distinctive splash of color to the complexion of city life.

Notice that nowhere have I said that the conclusions such individuals reach are *right*. What's more important is being able to see how, even if you think their conclusions are wrong, these conclusions are reached *because of an infusion of new information which in conditions of secularity may swiftly do its work*. And it may do its work even while many of the values of the small town are retained and while the believer slipping into doubt in the city greatly regrets what is happening rather than welcoming it.

With the deepened capacity for empathy that their own religions teach them to cultivate (and that is, in any case, itself a consequence of our culture's increasing pluralistic secularity), those who still believe, even if saddened thereby, should by now be able see how what appears to be nonresistant doubt often really is.

Conclusions

Recall that at the end of the previous chapter we reached this first conditional conclusion:

> If [a perfectly loving God exists], then [no finite person is ever nonresistantly in a state of nonbelief in relation to the proposition that God exists].

As you can see, I've left its antecedent and consequent clearly marked.

The premise we've been examining in the present chapter, to see whether it stands up to scrutiny, is the following:

Some finite persons are or have been nonresistantly in a state of nonbelief in relation to the proposition that God exists.

Having determined that it is true, we are in a position to add a conclusion to the hiddenness argument, *for our new premise negates the consequent of the above conditional*. Carrying over the reasoning from both the two previous chapters, as symbolized at the end of Chapter 5, we can express what's going on here logically in this way (the new reasoning enabled by the present chapter appears in bold):

(1) If P then Q.
(2) If Q then R.
(3) If P then R (from 1 and 2).
(4) Not-R.
(5) Not-P (from 3 and 4).

The logic involved in our most recent reasoning is the same as that at work in a Chapter 1 example. A company employee infers that her company has not won the contract when she learns that the manager is crying in the bathroom. Having previously arrived at the conditional conclusion that if the contract has been won then the manager is smiling, she is now in a position to *negate the consequent* of that conditional with the observation that he is *not* smiling and draw the conclusion that the *antecedent* of that conditional is false too: the contract has not been won.

Just so, the premise from this chapter, which tells us that finite persons *have* nonresistantly failed to believe that God exists, negates the consequent of Chapter 5's conclusion, which was that if a perfectly loving God exists then no finite person is ever nonresistantly in a state of nonbelief in relation to the proposition that God exists. Because the consequent of this proposition is false, it follows that the antecedent is false too: no perfectly loving God exists. It *must* be so, given that, as we saw in Chapter 1, the truth of the consequent is a *necessary condition* of the truth of the antecedent in any conditional. The antecedent can't be true unless the consequent is too—this is part of what any conditional proposition says—and here we've found the consequent to be false.

Remember what we have learned about arguments: if you think a couple of premises having the form of (3) and (4) just above are true and see that another proposition follows from them on the iron rails of logic, you have to accept that third proposition as true too or compromise what makes you a member of *H. sapiens*—your reason. Well, we've learned that perfect love has—via openness—a certain belief-related consequence. And we've also seen that the latter is not borne out by the actual world. So we have to conclude that the actual world is not the product of perfect love: no perfectly loving God exists.

This new conclusion carries quite a punch. But not as big a punch as the third and final conclusion we'll be able to draw after Chapter 7.

CHAPTER 7

MUST A GOD BE LOVING?

The question I've made my title in this seventh chapter has, as it were, been staring at us since this book began. We started work on the hiddenness argument's reasoning back in Chapter 4 with the assumption that a God *would* be loving, saying that we'd come back later to the question whether that is in fact the case. Well, later is now.

Why did we wait? I might have made this chapter the first in our series on the details of the hiddenness argument's reasoning instead of the last, but I decided not to do so for a variety of reasons. One reason is that only now can we see how important that premise is. Indeed, everything hangs on it. (Because of this, some might say that *here* we have the "main premise" of the argument.) Having seen that no perfectly loving God exists, if we also determine that God *would have to be* perfectly loving...well, then we're left with no option but to conclude that God does not exist.

That should be enough to concentrate our minds as we delve into the issue at hand—thus completing our survey of the approach "from above."

Perfection

When I first introduced the emphasis on love in *Divine Hiddenness and Human Reason,* some responded with the suggestion that I had thereby restricted the hiddenness argument's force to Christianity. Christians clearly teach that God is love, but this isn't—or isn't as obviously—the case for other theistic traditions. Islam emphasizes divine mercy and compassion, which may in some ways be related to love but don't amount to the same thing. And Judaism seems to get along with a God who—especially after the Holocaust—may be severely criticized and regarded as somewhat *deficient* in love. There's a moving story, associated with Elie Wiesel, of Jewish rabbis in Auschwitz putting God on trial, finding "Him" guilty, and then going to evening prayers. So it looks as though someone could be a theist, believing in God, without being committed to the claim that God is perfectly loving.

What should we make of this? Well, to get to the bottom of things, we need to disentangle the two distinct issues begging for attention here and treat them separately. One issue is whether God, even as the ultimate Person, might be other than perfectly loving. Another is whether God might be *im*perfect and *limited* and indeed *less* than ultimate in ways that include a deficiency in love. The second issue, therefore, involves some resistance to my assumption that religious investigation ought to be governed by the framework concept of ultimism discussed in Chapter 2. It really amounts to a request that we take a closer look at that, to make sure we're not buying into it too easily.

So let's do that. Our question in this first section of the chapter is accordingly the following: Might Godhood get along without personal perfection? One way I could proceed here involves an attempt to undermine reasons for saying so—for example, the reason provided by the behavior of those Jewish rabbis. Perhaps we could say that religiously committed people who permit themselves to rail against God, as even the Psalmist did, are trying to hold together in an imperfect finite way two things: (i) the depth of human suffering and how upset it should make us, if we have any decency at all, and (ii) the sense that somehow all shall be well, given by a *simultaneous* tendency to place all human experience into the ultimate frame of reference provided by religion. People in this position might say things about God that *seem* to imply God is limited and imperfect when in fact all we're seeing is a reflection of their attempt to enter deeply into what it is to be human and to respect the humanity of others.

I'm not sure this way of proceeding will work. Though I think it has some merit, it could leave even diligent rational inquirers unsure. In any case, it appears that some people really do think of God as limited and imperfect, if only because thinking that way has seemed to them to promise God an escape from rebuke in the face of terrible things that happen in the world. (I note in passing that this is probably an untrustworthy promise: how weak and ignorant would a *god* have to be to have, for allowing the Holocaust, the excuse "I couldn't do anything about it"?) Let's see what happens when we assume that this sort of thinking can indeed be found in the world of theistic religion, broadly conceived. In particular, do we then have to give up our framework concept of ultimism?

I don't think so. For one thing, that thinking could just be confused. Not everything one finds in the world of theistic religion accurately reflects its governing idea—take, for example, the *really* limiting notion that God is an old man in in the sky with a long white beard. This confuses the *idea* of God with a child's *image* of God. It also confuses a spiritual reality with a physical one, located in space. It is duly transcended by most theists who grow up a bit, religiously speaking. But that confusion is still found in the broader world of theism! So it's important to ask: Might *any* limitations imported into the idea of God similarly confuse?

One reason for saying so is that a God has to be worthy of worship, and a God that's less than ultimate would not be thus worthy. Already in the days of the ancient Greeks you'll find thinkers saying things like this. The philosopher Xenophanes, for example, sniffs at the Greek gods children today still learn about in school, saying that *his* god—who, he might have said, deserves the upper-case "G"—unlike *those* gods is worthy of worship. (It's instructive to find that what distinguishes Xenophanes' deity from those others is its omni-properties and therefore its striking similarity to the traditional God of theism, who is the ultimate Person.) If it's part of the very *idea* of God that God is worthy of worship, then it seems that nothing less than ultimacy will do when we consider how to think about God, for worship implies an absolutely unrestricted awe and devotion.

The point about worship is forceful, but I think it's best to locate it in the context of a couple of broader points about *religious experience* and *the evolution of religion*. It's precisely the sense of an absolutely limitless richness that most makes me want to apply the term "religious" to an experience. There has to be *some* term for experiences and ideas that want to burst all limits; what would it be if not "religious"? Such experiences are commonly what you'll find mystics talking about (or claiming they can't talk about, precisely because of their ultimistic qualities), and the founders of religions are often mystics. So the reasons for locating God within an ultimistic frame of reference are adding up.

But, you'll say, weren't lots of influential religions from times gone by, such as ancient Greek religion, pretty clearly non-ultimistic? This is where the point about religion's evolution kicks in. By the time we get to contemporary theism we've come a long way from those ancient traditions. And as theism gets discussed, in various streams of discussion, both philosophical and theological, over a couple of thousand years, its ultimistic properties become ever more clear and distinct. You don't even have to think that such changes mark improvements to see that there *are such changes*, which affect what people are putting forward for discussion when they say "Let's discuss the existence of God." Notice, for example, how both philosophers and theologians have greeted the work of "new atheists" such as Richard Dawkins by saying that the hugely complex but not ultimate supernatural designer of the universe he has sought to disprove *isn't really God*.

Given that such is the case, all we need in order properly to discuss theism within an ultimistic frame of reference in this book, and thus to assume that Godhood can't get along without perfection, is some reason not to rock the boat. A reason to keep steering the boat in the same ultimistic direction would also be nice. I think we get both from some more specific reflection on theism in western philosophy.

Philosophy, I remind you, is what we're doing in this book: this is a philosophical work. And philosophy has had limited use for limited gods. Figures in the history of the subject who have woven the idea of God into their philosophical work—take, for example, Leibniz and Descartes, among the greatest—have treated God as providing an *ultimate* explanation for how things go. Here we see at least metaphysical ultimacy. Consider again Richard Dawkins's god. Even if there is a really powerful supernatural designer, it wouldn't evidently provide a stopping point for explanation. If it doesn't do so, philosophy is going to keep looking. And at least a better candidate for metaphysical ultimacy, some have been saying, is the traditional theistic God, whose ultimistic properties of omnipotence, omniscience, and so on make it impossible for *such* a Being's existence to be explained by something outside itself.

So much for metaphysical ultimacy. As noted in Chapter 2, *axiological* ultimacy (unsurpassably great inherent value) has generally been in the background, and was made explicit by Anselm's that-than-which-a-greater-cannot-be-thought. This sort of ultimacy too has been regarded as doing philosophical work—for example, in ethics or moral philosophy. Something similar might be said about *soteriological* ultimacy (unsurpassable importance in relation to our own good). But a perhaps more significant reason for tying theism to soteriological ultimacy will quickly be seen by anyone who has reflected deeply on the nature of religion, and noticed how it always promises its adherents that they're on the best, most important path they could be on. (By the way, here we see why even a non-ultimate God might not escape the hiddenness argument: its soteriological ultimacy might require that even if limited in other ways, it was not limited in love.)

By this point, however, some readers may fear that we've veered from philosophy into religious studies. Why should a *philosopher* care if theism comes with all these bells and whistles, so long as it can do some philosophical work? Why *must* theism in philosophy be linked to all three sorts of ultimacy?

My basic answer is that among philosophy's jobs is the job of doing philosophy *of religion*. Philosophers these days will be found doing philosophy of science, philosophy of language, philosophy of art, and various other such "philosophy-ofs." Philosophy of religion is among them. In doing such work, philosophers are trying to arrive at a clear understanding of the central concepts and claims from these domains of human life. Granted, they may also seek to make use of what they learn to address deep problems in the other and central areas of philosophy: namely, metaphysics, ethics, and epistemology (concerned with fundamental issues about what there is, how we should live, and how we can know, respectively). But philosophers don't—or at least shouldn't—just rove like conceptual bandits in the territories of science and art and religion, looking to rip them off for the benefit of, say, ethics or metaphysics. They want to understand scientific and religious and other ideas in their own right, seeing things as they are in these areas of human life, while also considering what they may contribute to a wider philosophical understanding.

Given this balanced understanding of the philosophical task, a philosopher should care about the fact that theism is a religious idea, and about the axiological and soteriological dimensions this brings into view, and not just strip off its metaphysical and more straightforwardly explanatory components, suggesting that these alone are properly called "theism" or "the concept of God."

But there's another point here too. In doing philosophy we need to think not only about how ideas have developed so far in this or that domain of human life but also about how we can best develop them *further*. I suggest that from religion's perspective and its own, philosophy would do well to make the ultimistic character of much religious thinking even clearer than it sometimes has been so far, taking the idea of a religious or divine reality further in an ultimistic direction by making its ultimistic character fully explicit along all three of the dimensions I have mentioned, metaphysical, axiological, and soteriological. The idea of a reality ultimate in all three ways is a beautiful idea, arguably the most impressive religion has yet delivered; it also, as we've seen, most fully satisfies the aspirations of religious experience and worship. Moreover, there's ever so much more work to be done in thinking about *the various ways in which it might be realized*, and if it should turn out to be true, that would have enormous philosophical ramifications. (If instead it should turn out that no such reality exists, there'll be plenty of time left for philosophers to take up the theme of sub-ultimacy.)

Thinking about theism within this frame of reference means taking theism as *one* way ultimism might be true and fleshing it out accordingly. And that means assuming that when theists talk about God as a person, they mean that God is the *greatest possible* person. When they say that God exists, they should be taken to mean that the greatest possible person exists. Philosophers—as well as anyone inclined to say that they're concerned to know not just whether some god exists but whether *God* exists—will rightly be very interested in any test of that claim of the sort that the hiddenness argument represents.

Omni-Love

So the equation "theism = personal ultimism" is justified philosophically, and given the nature of religious experience and worship it is justified in purely religious terms as well. This being the case, we should say that a God would indeed display personal perfection. But what about the first issue above, from which we sought to disentangle the one we've just been talking about: Does personal perfection really entail perfect love?

Here we need to think about the qualities a perfect or unsurpassably great person would have to possess. (Contrary to what some of my critics have said, such reflection—and not just a Christian prejudice—is what lay behind my claim in *Divine Hiddenness and Human Reason* that a God would be perfectly loving.) For a philosopher, all the omni-properties—omnipotence, omniscience, and so on—will come tumbling into view fairly quickly when this subject is raised. But perfect love is not always among them. Even omnibenevolence, as we saw in Chapter 4, which does get a nod from philosophers, doesn't really get at what's distinctive about love. The "more" here has to do with a deep sharing valued for its own sake, which is tied to personal relationship. An unsurpassable love, for various reasons, would seek meaningful, conscious relationship with the beloved; it would always at least be open to sharing *itself* in such relationship.

So why hasn't omni-love understood in this way always made it onto the philosophical lists? And should this trouble the hiddenness arguer?

I think the correct answer to the first question will mention, again, how much things have changed in the recent history of our culture. Men can talk about love these days. Most philosophers have been men, and the thinking men who did philosophy were usually more comfortable with "hard" concepts such as those having to do with *power* and *control*. Omnipotence. Now *there's* a concept you can get your analytical teeth into! Many philosophers even today seem more comfortable with power than with love, but things are changing. So expect to see love more commonly discussed in philosophy of religion textbooks of the future.

If this answer is even close to the truth, then the answer to the second question is also clear: hiddenness arguers needn't be troubled in the slightest by the fact that omni-love doesn't always appear on traditional lists of God's attributes. At least this is the case if—perhaps better than ever with our twenty-first-century eyes—we can see that omni-love *belongs* on the list given that the value of love in persons is no less obvious than the value of knowledge or power. So I ask: Can you see this?

Here's one way to think about it. Bring before your mind the concept of the greatest possible person—a person so great that none could be greater—and suppose also that this person has created a world including finite persons. Think about this person's attributes. Now either your conception already embraces perfect love toward those other persons among its attributes or it doesn't. If it does, I've made my case. If it doesn't, then ask yourself what is the result of mentally *adding* perfect love to the collection of attributes you've conceived. I predict that the result is an improvement, a more impressive person. (After all, don't we admire in people an openness to deep sharing with others, for their sake and also for its own? Isn't this a virtue we cultivate?) But then you hadn't yet conceived the greatest possible person before. The greatest possible person, whatever else it may be, has to be perfectly loving. Indeed, it would be natural to expect its power and knowledge to be expressed on behalf of love, and certainly not in competition with it.

Not incidentally, there is a nice fit between this claim, which really concerns only *axiological* ultimacy, and what we have to say about *soteriological* ultimacy in a world created by God. As we've seen, theism, to count as a religious idea, must have soteriological content: it must be possible for the value of the ultimate to be in some way communicated to finite persons and the world, if we're working with a religious notion. And it's easy to see how this could be the case in a world in which God is ultimate, if positive transformation were brought about through personal relationship between finite persons and God. Now love seeks just such relationship. So there is a match between axiology and soteriology here, as well as a religious and philosophical grounding for the hiddenness argument's emphasis on God's love as entailing openness to relationship.

But we should still test the claim that personal perfection entails perfect love. What arguments can we use to do so? These will be arguments for a loveless God, since there's no chance that God would be loving but less than *perfectly* loving—loving in some more limited way. Within an ultimistic frame of reference, it's all or nothing: because God must be perfect in every way, either God is perfectly loving or God is not loving at all. How might we argue that the latter condition of lovelessness at least *might* be God's, for all we know? And do such arguments have any force?

(i) Perhaps the best way to argue for this conclusion would involve premises that stress the great differences there must be between the persons we are and the person God is, precisely because in thinking about God we're trying to conceive an *ultimate* person. One such argument will say that the sort of sharing, relational love I have in mind is important in human life and should indeed be cultivated by us because we need it to get along with each other and advance the human project, as well as to grow and flourish individually: there is, for example, ever so much we can learn from each other in sharing relationships. But God doesn't need to evolve and grow, or to get along with others in order to survive. God doesn't need love to flourish. God is the necessarily existing, perfectly good, and complete originator and sustainer of all things! So the reasons we have for saying that love enhances human life don't apply to God. Though it may sound odd, God can therefore be the *greatest possible* person without having this attribute of love which happens to make *our* lives so much better.

Such an argument might have some weight if its reasons for saying love is good were the *only* reasons. But they're not. For one thing, these reasons all stress love's *instrumental* value in human life—what it's good *for*. Isn't love also *intrinsically* valuable, good in itself? And if so, mightn't there be a very different reason for saying God would have it too? A person who's open and sharing, willing to give of herself in relationship, has a quality we admire, as well as desire for ourselves; we rightly think it's good in itself for a person to be this way, and not just that we can *get* or *give* something by being loving. Consider for a moment this sharing, relational love in its various human manifestations: the love of friends, the love of siblings, the love of spouses. It is not only because of what it *produces* in the way of happiness or personal and societal growth that we value it.

Another way of showing up this weakness in the argument focuses on the love of parents for their children. We rightly think there's something *intrinsically* amiss if either parent is unwilling to share of himself or herself in a close relationship with their children, because there is something noticeably amiss here even if we assume that the benefits the parent is thus unable to make available to his or her children will not be that great or will be outweighed by harms avoided. The counterpart point is of course that something intrinsically is *right* if they *do* possess such dispositions. Now if God is a person and God has brought into the world finite persons capable of relationship with God and indeed fulfilled only by it, then something very like the parent–child relation exists between God and finite persons. And then also, given the point made above, we should say that God is intrinsically better than God would otherwise be if God is loving toward finite persons.

(ii) Another argument against the idea that the greatest possible person would have to be loving says that love of the sort I have in mind is to a considerable extent a matter of *emotion and desire*, and that in God, the greatest possible Person, these things will not be found. God wouldn't feel the pain of rejection or the joy of reunion or the need for connection with another person. It follows that love would not be found in God.

This argument might have found some advocates back in the day when certain ancient Greek notions—such as the idea that change signals imperfection—held more sway over western minds. Emotion and desire, as well as phenomena bound up with them, involve change. And so an ancient Greek might have held that they can't be found in the greatest possible Person. Some early Christian thinkers agreed, and ascribed to God the quality of immutability (changelessness). But philosophers today tend for their various reasons to reject the idea that there's something wrong with God if God experiences change. This idea might make more sense if God didn't create anything, but if God creates a changing world, isn't something wrong if God can't respond to the world sensitively and skilfully and in light of its needs—all of which presupposes change? In any case, why can't we just say that God is unchangingly powerful and loving and good and so on, allowing the ways in which such unfailing characteristics are *manifested* to change? Long story short: the present argument would be a non-starter today if it depended on the ancient Greek assumption.

But what other leg does it have to stand on when it says God can't feel emotion or desire? Especially at a time when the old patriarchal assumptions which had some men frowning on the "femininity" of emotion and desire are (mostly) behind us, why would we say such a thing? Indeed, if God is the greatest possible Person, mightn't we expect *super*-emotions in God: depths of joy and springs of empathy no finite being could ever fathom?

But perhaps the reference to "need" in connection with emotion and desire provides a clue to what could support the argument: if God *needs* something, then it seems God must be deficient in some way: there must at the very least be, at a certain time, something good from which God would benefit but which God then lacks. And this can't ever be so if God is unsurpassably great.

The leg here proffered for the argument to stand on is weak. For emotion and desire don't entail need in this sense. Trivially, what God desires might ceaselessly and uninterruptedly be achieved, so that God never suffers need. More substantially and relevantly, God could be overflowing in loving kindness and joyfully inviting all to share in the love of God and also thinking it good for such to be the case and doing what God can do to facilitate success in such a project, and thus clearly loving all creatures, *even if* the remainder of the infinitely rich life of God were such as to make it impossible for God to suffer unhappiness over this or that finite response.

(iii) A different sort of argument we might try for the conclusion that a perfect personal being need not be loving in my sense says that there is another sense in which God has always been said to be loving, and that such love is enough. This is the endlessly and selflessly giving love of *agape*. The love I've been talking about, so it may be said, is rather the love of *eros*, which religious thinkers have always found less attractive as a candidate for Godly love.

Here we must beware of a baseless appeal to authority, and also of a move we might call "argument by labeling." What has always been said might be (and often is) flat wrong. Moreover labels don't always fit, and—flipping the coin over—*may* fit despite questionable associations they have picked up in some quarters. Eros it is natural to associate with the aching need of sexual love, but if we take it instead to be about seeking relationship with another *for its own sake*, as the philosopher and religious thinker Robert Merrihew Adams has recently shown it is possible to do, then there's no reason to deny that it would ever be found in God. Quite the contrary.

Another and related problem with labels, especially where we're dealing with matters as subtle as love, is that the divisions they enforce are often a bit artificial, untrue to the reality we mean to depict. As Adams suggests, agape and eros would go together in the best love, with a desire for relationship being in part a desire to benefit the person one loves *through* relationship. Finally, it's worth noting that even agape or benevolence alone, as I've argued in *Divine Hiddenness and Human Reason*, might already lead God to facilitate a relationship with creatures—think of all that God could give to them by doing so!—and so we might not even need anything linkable to eros in the hiddenness argument in order for that argument to make its case.

(iv) A last argument I want to consider here takes us back to the notion of mystery: an unsurpassably great Person one could not hope to understand, but in that case *who knows* whether the love required for the hiddenness argument to work is going to be found in it? We should suspend judgment about this matter instead of forming any definite view about it.

The distinction between ultimism and theism is helpful here. Though something like this reasoning might be persuasive when addressed to talk about bare ultimism, here we're dealing with the theistic *elaboration* of ultimism, which adds personal details. The suggestion we are entertaining when we consider the idea that there is a personal God is that the ultimate is a *person*, and so we need to start thinking about what an unsurpassable Person would be like instead of taking it all back and retreating into mystery. The move to mystery is in fact quite inimical to the context of inquiry in which the claim that there is a personal God is addressed by thinking people. It is also belied by all the *other* attributes that theists are content to have applied to God and precisely defined, such as omnipotence, omniscience, and omnibenevolence. Why shrink just here, when in the same spirit that generated those attributes we want to add love? It would be arbitrary and quite unjustified to do so.

God

The available responses to arguments we have used to test the claim that personal perfection entails perfect love are therefore unanimous in their verdict: such arguments all fail to overthrow that claim. Since we began this discussion already possessing some powerful intuitive grounds to accept that claim, and also to accept that Godhood entails personal perfection, we are now in a position to endorse the following premise of the hiddenness argument:

If no perfectly loving God exists, then God does not exist.

Put this together with the conclusion reached by the end of the previous chapter,

No perfectly loving God exists,

and what do you have, so clearly that no explanations of the logic involved are necessary? An answer to the fundamental question about God:

God does not exist.

But it would be good, now that we have reached the end of our exposition of the hiddenness argument, to put all of the bits of its logical skeleton together, to see exactly where and how this third and last conclusion follows from previous reasoning (our last move is put in bold). Having already used the variables "P," "Q," and "R," let's go one step further down the alphabet and use "S" to stand for our final conclusion, that God does not exist.

(1) If P then Q.
(2) If Q then R.
(3) If P then R (from 1 and 2).
(4) Not-R.
(5) Not-P (from 3 and 4).
(6) If not-P then S.
(7) S (from 5 and 6).

And now adding a body to that skeleton:

(1) If a perfectly loving God exists, then there exists a God who is always open to a personal relationship with any finite person.
(2) If there exists a God who is always open to a personal relationship with any finite person, then no finite person is ever nonresistantly in a state of nonbelief in relation to the proposition that God exists.
(3) If a perfectly loving God exists, then no finite person is ever nonresistantly in a state of nonbelief in relation to the proposition that God exists (from 1 and 2).
(4) Some finite persons are or have been nonresistantly in a state of nonbelief in relation to the proposition that God exists.
(5) No perfectly loving God exists (from 3 and 4).
(6) If no perfectly loving God exists, then God does not exist.
(7) God does not exist (from 5 and 6).

CHAPTER 8

THE CHALLENGE

The hiddenness argument helped to tip the scales for me at a critical period in my life. Perhaps it will do the same for you, if you are wondering whether a person-like God—the God of theism—exists. But I don't assume that every well-functioning intellect, after reading the previous chapters of this book, will be pointing unwaveringly toward atheism.

Nonetheless there is a new challenge to be met. Notice that this challenge does not presuppose any general theory as to what's required for a belief to be properly held, such as the idea that one's beliefs must all be based on adequate *public evidence* to be justified. Saying that one ought not to believe a proposition that has been disproven by public evidence does not imply that what one *should* believe is to be determined entirely by reference to public evidence. Perhaps some beliefs that are not thus disproven will properly be grounded in private experiences. As it happens, I will be making room for private religious experiences in a few moments.

Let's briefly take stock. The hiddenness argument's inferences are watertight: all its conclusions follow just as indicated at the end of the previous chapter. That is one of the benefits of using a form of argument in which conclusions follow with necessity if they follow at all. As we've noted, logicians call it *deductive* reasoning. When this sort of argument is used, you can just *see* that the conclusions follow (when they do). No philosopher in twenty years has questioned this for the hiddenness argument.

So it all comes down to the premises. If you have interpreted them correctly and they seem to you to be true, and if moreover you have nothing to set against that, then those premises should lead you straight to the conclusion that theism is false. Two main issues are raised here: whether you have read the premises correctly, and whether you have something to set against—by which to oppose or counter—their seeming truth, if that's how they strike you when correctly interpreted. Let's start with the first issue. The second will occupy us for the remainder of the chapter.

Misinterpretations

Most of the points I want to make in this section should feel like reminders, but it will be good to have them before us—the argument has often been misinterpreted in its short 25-year history. It is really a fairly simple and straightforward argument, and it would be ironic if all the efforts I have made to explain and defend it should be taken as evidence that it is very complex, or controversial even among non-theists, or that it deals in the obscure: this too would be a misinterpretation. But because the argument's premises have so often been subject to misinterpretation, let me take some time to underline the main mistakes that might be made here but should scrupulously be avoided.

(i) The argument does not say, in its first premise, that the openness to relationship of a loving God would be displayed toward *us* or toward *human beings*. This is more important than it may seem, since if it is thought that a perfectly loving God would have to create human beings, then it will mistakenly be supposed that facts *about human beings* determine whether God has reason to permit nonresistant nonbelief or not. Although theology, which by its very nature is able to assume that God exists (and therefore that God opted to create human beings), can legitimately suppose this, philosophy cannot. Philosophy has to be open to the possibility that facts about human beings determine only that a God would not create human beings!

(ii) Unsurpassable love, as understood in the argument, is not reducible to unsurpassable benevolence but also involves valuing personal relationship for its own sake.

(iii) Not just any sort of relationship that might seem to merit the label "personal" can be substituted for what the argument is talking about: love of the sort that takes us beyond benevolence and is clearly a great-making property values for its own sake a conscious, reciprocal relationship with the one loved.

(iv) The argument nowhere states or implies that God should *bring about* a personal relationship between God and finite persons but only that God would be perpetually *open* to such relationship.

(v) The argument nowhere states or implies that God's *presence* would be felt by all, let alone felt overwhelmingly, but only that all who are nonresistant will believe that God exists.

(vi) Nothing in the argument gives credence to the idea that what finite persons would be able to do when participating in relationship with God "just by trying" would be *easy* or, more generally, that participating in personal relationship with God would be a joy ride. More generally still, we should note that there can be innumerable *styles* of personal relationship with God and that it is an error to focus on a single troublesome style, suggesting that the hiddenness argument is committed to it.

(vii) The argument does not claim that God would intervene in the lives of nonresistant believers, perhaps disruptively, to give them evidence sufficient for belief, but rather states that if God exists *there will never be any nonresistant nonbelievers.*

(viii) It will not suffice to refute the hiddenness argument if one can show that reflective *doubters* in the western world *today* are all resisting belief in God. I think that's false too, but what makes the relevant premise of the argument clearly true is that the category of nonresistant nonbelievers the argument can work with is so broad, including not just reflective doubters but also those who never have had a real chance to *think* about God; and not just people living today but all finite persons capable of believing in God and responding positively to such belief *who have ever lived*—which of course takes us back very far indeed into evolutionary history.

If the argument is approached in a philosophical spirit of truth-seeking, and such interpretive errors are avoided, then I think its premises will seem quite clearly acceptable.

Objections

So what might you have to set against that apparent clear acceptability, if anything? A natural first suggestion is that there may be further objections to be considered. Each time we discussed one of the premises, we went through a number of objections—reasons for questioning whether the premise was true. In each case I argued that the objections were unsuccessful. But might we have missed something?

Well, if someone can think of an important further objection that needs to be considered, then indeed, as a truth-seeker, they ought to consider it. And if the objection seems successful, then indeed you'll have something to set against the premise to which it objects. But I'm pessimistic about any additional objections doing better than those we've considered. Why is that?

There's more than one reason. First, the objections examined here are representative of objections raised over twenty years by philosophers of various stripes—many of them highly motivated to defeat the hiddenness argument if it could be done. I've argued that none is successful. This doesn't particularly surprise me given a second point: the premises of the hiddenness argument are all highly plausible to begin with. As I mentioned in Chapter 1, arguers should try to use premises that will be convincing for those in their audience who consider them with openness to the truth. And I think that is often the case for those who see the hiddenness argument for the first time. In such circumstances objections still need to be considered, but this is not because the premises are in some way doubtful but because we want to be sure we haven't missed anything. At a certain point in inquiry, really plausible premises that withstand relevant tests simply need to be accepted; otherwise inquiry can't proceed. At a certain point, indeed, you may switch from being a truth-seeker to being a truth-*denier* or truth-*delayer* if you keep on demanding consideration of extra objections.

So I myself think the consideration of objections we've undertaken is sufficient. But that's just me. If you think there are important objections I've missed, then by all means examine them. However, here comes my third point. Though we won't be discussing specific objections any further here, I *can* identify certain general considerations that objections tend to bump into, disintegrating on contact, of which you ought to take account if further objections occur to you. In the past twenty years I've noticed these general points become relevant again and again, and by now I'm pretty sure that any new objection will meet its demise by the time all of them have been mobilized. So I'd suggest that truth-seekers anxious about new objections not forget them and indeed be ready to run through them if and when fresh objections are put forward. Most of these points have already emerged in previous discussion. But it will, again, be good to remind ourselves what they are and get them together in one place.

(i) *The benefits of cultural evolution.* The value of relational love in persons, the place of openness to relationship in such love, the actual existence of nonresistant nonbelief—claims made about such things by the argument's premises are strongly supported by what human beings have learned over time about our evolutionary history, the lives of people on the other side of the globe, the importance of empathy, the nature of mature personal relationships, and so on through such things as science (including social science), the movement for gender equality, and the explosion of Web-based social media. (The only remaining claim of the argument, that openness to conscious relationship at a time is incompatible with preventing the belief that you exist from being at that time formed by the one you love, is perfectly obvious.) So be sure that new objections don't just fly in the face of some of these things we've learned. Objections deriving from religious traditions formed *prior* to such positive cultural evolution are especially liable to do so. (Take, for example, the idea that God is a King exalted on high who need not deign to interact with us "his" unworthy subjects.) Members of such traditions who are attracted to such objections may accordingly find themselves needing to check their credentials as truth-seekers—as distinct from their credentials as loyal Muslims, Christians, or Jews—even more often than usual.

(ii) *Relationship-compatible goods.* Many objections to the hiddenness argument propose *goods* which it's thought a God might pursue and which appear incompatible in some way with what the argument claims God would do. Such objections need to be considered in light of a point about relationship-compatible goods that applies in a specific way some of what I've just mentioned under the previous point. If God has created a world which prominently features finite persons, and if God is to be regarded as perfectly loving toward them, then the goods God seeks to realize in that world will be compatible with openness to loving relationship with them, just as the goods that a loving mother seeks to realize in and through her life are ones she regards as compatible with such openness to her children. If you're a loving person, the structure of your projects cannot be unaffected by your commitments to those you love. (This is a perfectly general point.) To see the plausibility and importance of this idea about relationship-compatible goods in relation to proposed objections, it helps to see that no real restriction comes with it: if God is unsurpassably great then in an important sense *all good is in God,* and there could hardly be a better world than one that permitted the good that is in God to be ever more fully shared with finite creatures.

(iii) A *developmental view of relationship with God.* People sometimes think a relationship with God would be a somewhat flat one-dimensional thing. It's almost as though once you're there, you're there; the trajectory of your life has been completed. So everything interesting you do as a growing, developing person had better be squeezed in *prior* to getting there. This is a highly misleading picture, though it can make some objections to the hiddenness argument seem more plausible than they really are for those who are misled by it. If God would be an unsurpassably great Person, then God would be endlessly rich and beautiful and interesting and the process of knowing God would indeed *have* to be a *process*, with endless stages of development as you grasp ever more of the beauty and wonder of God. It may sound odd to hear an atheistic philosopher say such things. But remember that I'm a *philosopher*, and as such my job is to get as clear as I can on what people really are talking about when they talk about God. Nothing less than what is described here could possibly do the trick. And how is it relevant to possible new objections? Well, objections to the hiddenness argument proposing goods that allegedly require someone somewhere not to believe in God are often of a type that can be accommodated within relationship with God *precisely because of how much the latter would have to encompass*. You want room for inquiry? There will always be more to know about God. You want opportunities for free choices as to the nature of your character? There will be endless opportunities to choose to be more like God. And so on. Truth-seekers will carefully seek to determine whether new objections can be countered in this way.

(iv) *Secondary hiddenness*. As a young man putting forward for publication my manuscript on *Divine Hiddenness and Human Reason*, I was pleased as punch to have the respected philosopher William P. Alston, then General Editor for the Cornell University Press series *Cornell Studies in the Philosophy of Religion*, going through my text with a fine-toothed comb. I was even more pleased to see his mostly positive reactions. Perhaps his most positive individual reaction appeared next to what I had to say about what I'm here calling "secondary hiddenness." In the margin he wrote: "Very powerful." My idea made use of what some mystics have called "the dark night of the soul." These mystics believe in God, consider themselves to be in a relationship with God, but find themselves going through a period of spiritual darkness or aridity in which God seems far away. This period is invariably thought to serve some deep moral or spiritual good of the sort people have used to argue that God would be hidden in the *deeper* way—"primary hiddenness"—opposed by the hiddenness argument. I claimed that since there was room even *within* a relationship with God for this sort of divine withdrawal—for a secondary kind of hiddenness—and since it would in a variety of cases accomplish all that the primary sort of hiddenness with its greater relationship-related costs was said to realize, there was no need for the latter in those cases. This still seems to me to be a powerful point capable of handling on its own many of the objections to hiddenness reasoning that have been or may be advanced.

Two last points on objections. First, an objection that succeeds in getting a truth-seeker all the way to doubt about a premise of the hiddenness argument (as opposed to disbelief) is good enough to prevent her from rationally concluding that God does not exist on the basis of that argument; but even coming to be in doubt about *each* premise of the argument will not be enough to allow someone who was formerly a believer in God to rationally retain such belief, if she has nothing else to bring to the table. What such a believer needs from an objection in order to retain her belief in such circumstances is, in addition, a good reason to think that at least one premise of the argument is *false*. Otherwise, finding herself no more than in doubt about each premise as she considers it, she will be in doubt also about the conclusion that the conjunction of those premises entails—rationally unsure whether God exists or not.

Second, when all else fails, opponents of the hiddenness argument sometimes develop the objection that there might very well be goods *unknown* to us that require hiddenness, for the sake of which God would permit it; but if the hiddenness arguer has done a good job and has led you to think her premises clearly true, then this move fails. That's because from what some of those premises allow us to conclude, namely, that a loving God *would not* permit nonresistant nonbelief, it deductively follows that there are no goods, known or unknown, such that for their sake God *might* do so. So *that* should seem clearly true to you too—after all, it evidently follows from what you regard as clearly true—and thus the latest objection has to be ruled a logical foul. The objector is assuming that you are not in a position to make this deductive inference—otherwise why would he say that there *might be* those unknown goods?—when in fact you are.

Counter-Arguments

But objections aren't the only sort of thing that someone might think should be set against the appearance of truth in the premises of the hiddenness argument. There are also counter-arguments. Counter-arguments, as understood here, are not the same as objections. An objection to a premise of the hiddenness argument tries to provide a reason for thinking that premise false or for being in doubt about whether it's true. Either way, the premise can be prevented from doing its job (though remember the qualification from two paragraphs ago). But a counter-argument is a *separate* argument—or collection of arguments—*for* the existence of God which, it's thought, offsets or "counters" the force of the hiddenness argument. If you had such an argument at your disposal, then you could say that the premises of the hiddenness argument all look good while, all things considered, not accepting them all as true. Indeed, you could say that the hiddenness argument appears totally convincing. For here—so you'll add—you have this *other* argument *for* God that seems totally convincing too. Of course, if the hiddenness argument does appear convincing, then even in this best-case scenario you'll still be left in doubt as to whether God exists, at least if all you have to go on are arguments. For you'll find yourself with a convincing argument on both sides. On the other hand, someone wondering whether she should make the move from agnosticism to atheism on the basis of the hiddenness argument would find, should she discover such a counter-argument, a good reason to stay put.

So is any such counter-argument available? I don't think so. And my reason isn't just that I find none of the arguments for the existence of God persuasive (after all, others may disagree). There's an important structural point here—a structural *impediment* to the success of this approach for anyone who finds the hiddenness argument persuasive and can't find a persuasive objection to it of the sort we were just discussing. This is that no similarly *deductive* argument for the existence of God is even being defended these days. The only arguments out there for a person-like God aspire to make it *probable* that such a being exists—they are, as a logician will say, *inductive* rather than deductive. There is, for example, the complex cumulative case put forward by my former supervisor at Oxford, Richard Swinburne, with the conclusion that God probably exists. Even if completely successful, such a case is going to be outweighed by a deductive argument for atheism with premises that seem clearly true even after objections have been considered, and with conclusions that clearly follow with necessity. This is one reason why I am happy to give the hiddenness argument a deductive form. Though I share a general sense in philosophy these days that successful deductive arguments for substantial conclusions are thin on the ground, *where they can be found* they are often very useful, intellectually. Indeed, given the relatively early stage of human inquiry we are presently in, and the worries attending it about future discoveries that might negatively affect present results, a convincing clear cut deductive case may sometimes be *needed* for a conclusion to be drawn with any confidence, and should be sought. I suggest that in the hiddenness argument we have found such a success story.

But someone may wonder whether there really are no deductive arguments for the existence of God that are being defended these days. What about the cosmological argument? Or the ontological argument? True enough. Such arguments are generally given a deductive form. But now we have another structural problem. For the (relevant) arguments being defended are not really arguments for the existence *of a person-like God.* All the most impressive deductive cosmological argument concludes is that there is a necessary being. Attempts to take such reasoning further and argue that the necessary being must be a personal God have never gained much support in philosophy. And the ontological argument merely concludes that a greatest possible being exists—a broad conclusion far closer to ultimism without elaboration than to its theistic elaboration.

Experience

We're asking what, if anything, a truth-seeker might find to set against the premises of the hiddenness argument, which we have discovered are very convincing. A new answer doesn't appeal to reasoning at all, of any kind. Instead, this very different answer appeals to *experiences apparently of God*. I would judge that the most popular ways of responding to the hiddenness argument today on the part of believers in God, both within philosophy and outside, will make at least some use of such an appeal. Can a truth-seeker do so without giving up her badge?

What exactly are we talking about here? Well, someone may, for example, have a powerful sense that God is present to them. Perhaps something like a majestic natural scene sensorily perceived and aesthetically impactful or interaction with other human beings will mediate it; perhaps not. Perhaps they just have a strong feeling that God is with them—maybe in a comforting or supporting or instructing mode—much as someone might have a strong sense that a person is behind them in a dark room without there being anything sensorily perceived in virtue of which they have this sense. Suppose that something of *this* sort causes someone to believe firmly that God exists and to infer that something must therefore be wrong with the hiddenness argument, even if they can't put their finger on it. Could such a move have intellectual integrity?

Unfortunately we also have to assume that this "someone" finds the hiddenness argument really convincing, and has no apparently powerful objections to raise against its premises. (Otherwise, her condition would already have been addressed a couple of sections back, when we were discussing objections.) And so it seems we again have reached, at best, a standoff. On the one side she has the hiddenness argument. On the other side she has her powerful experiences. It sounds like a tie, and so going with what experience suggests would be arbitrary and irrational, without something to break the tie. Doubt is the rational result for truth-seekers in cases such as this.

Perhaps it will be said that a simple non-inferential ground for belief of the sort that direct experience provides should win out over a complicated series of inferences of the sort we find in the hiddenness argument, which has multiple places where one could have gone wrong. But it is a mistake to say that the hiddenness argument is a very complicated argument. It is rather quite a simple argument which requires complicated discussion, given the various cultural factors that militate against a straightforward reading and evaluation. However, set that aside. For there are other problems here too, which make a theistic experience and its evaluation less simple and direct than they might initially seem. An experience apparently of a person-like God is quite a *specific and detailed* sort of experience. Clearly there are going to be other people as honest and careful and sensitive as our truth-seeker who have *different and contrary* experiences favoring a non-theistic religious proposition—one entailing that God does *not* exist. This is something that is getting increasingly more difficult to deny given recent cultural evolution, which has made it rather easy for us to get to know such people. Today theists may have Buddhist or Hindu or completely nonreligious friends whose experiences contradict their own. Since not all of these experiences can be delivering the truth, aren't they *all* untrustworthy in the absence of something *other* than experience to—as it were—break the tie? Notice that now the tie is between one experience and another, not between experience and the hiddenness argument, so this is a problem people who rely on theistic religious experience are going to encounter whether we bring atheistic arguments to the table or not.

This problem of experiential diversity can arise, it's interesting to note, not just between lives but within a single one too. And here also our wider and deeper exposure these days to diverse forms of religious life plays a role. A person may grow up in one form of religion and move to another contrary form of religion, finding herself with apparently validating experiences in both. Except for the "another contrary form of religion" part, something like this happened to me. At various times early in my life I had powerful theistic religious experiences. But since leaving theistic religion—indeed, after becoming an atheist—I have also at various times had powerful and unmistakeably religious experiences that had no distinctively theistic content at all. These latter experiences did not form in me any sort of religious belief, in part because of my awareness of the problem of religious experiential diversity, but they did make me more open to the possibility of a religious dimension to life. In my view, that is a good and already meaningful result for anyone who has religious experiences, but religious *belief* is harder to justify here.

Of course if someone has a powerful theistic religious experience and is caused by it to believe invincibly—she simply cannot help it—even though she previously had been convinced by an atheistic argument, we won't criticize her. But that's because in such circumstances, in which the point put forward is that one is powerless to prevent what has happened, someone's state of belief is *excused,* in something like the way actions may be excused when we are unable to control them, not because a *reason* has become available that justifies it.

Truthiness

In 2005, on his television show *The Colbert Report,* the great philosopher Stephen Colbert introduced a word he had just made up—"truthiness." He defined it as "truth that comes from the gut, not books." Not a great definition, perhaps: wasn't he thinking about *a quality possessed by* an apparent truth affirmed by the gut? But it's his word. Since Colbert was making fun of politicians and others who are selectively anti-intellectual or who trust their own feelings or may give in to their intellectual wishes far too easily, it's safe to assume that truthiness or attraction to it is for him not a good thing. The word became enormously popular and was chosen as the 16th annual Word of the Year in 2006 by the American Dialect Society, and defined by them as "the quality of preferring concepts or facts one wishes to be true, rather than concepts or facts known to be true." This sounds a lot like good old-fashioned wishful thinking. Here what one *wants* has come to the fore, which shows that gut feelings are often tied to *the desire that some proposition be true*. And such desires can be misleading. Maybe truth-seekers especially should be on their guard against confusing what they want to be true with what really is true, or at any rate best supported by the evidence, when considering their gut feelings.

I bring all this up because people will sometimes resist an argument such as the hiddenness argument because they have a "gut feeling" that the argument is wrong—and this even after finding nothing to fault in it. An interesting question worth asking is whether gut feelings should be regarded as untrustworthy by truth-seekers, because of the possible connection to wishful thinking already noted.

Certainly it's important to *ask* oneself whether one's gut feeling is merely the apprehension of truthiness. If so, it might very well not put one in touch with the truth, and should not be trusted. But there's actually a clear reason not to trust gut feelings in such religious matters. And this is the same reason we mentioned in connection with religious experience. There are other people as honest and careful and sensitive as you who have gut feelings that favor a proposition entailing that God does *not* exist. And so if we were to trust gut feelings non-arbitrarily, we'd have to say that they support a contradiction: "God exists and God does not exist." But no "evidence" that supports a contradiction should be trusted, since contradictions can't be true!

Because this problem has come up twice now, I'd be remiss if I didn't inform readers that the general topic of disagreement and what to do about it is today being hotly debated in epistemology, the area of philosophy concerned with what we can know and how. There is much talk of "the epistemology of disagreement." Unfortunately, however, the philosophers involved have not been able to come to any agreement about disagreement. No consensus is in sight. It's hard not to think that this should be unsettling for a truth-seeker looking on and wondering whether she can rationally trust her gut feelings on the question whether God exists.

Truthing

In my life I have at various times been a theist, an atheist, and an agnostic. Though I didn't know the label growing up, a theist is what I was. I believed in a person-like God, and if you had explained the terms to me, I certainly would have agreed that God was ultimate in all three of the ways embraced by ultimism: metaphysically, axiologically, and soteriologically. So I guess I was also, without knowing it, a personalizing ultimist (or an ultimizing personalist—take your pick).

When in my early twenties biblical criticism and philosophy turned my world upside down (or rightside up—take your pick), I suppose I was for a time an agnostic, though my state of mind was more fluctuating than that might suggest: I went back and forth between belief and doubt, and then later between *dis*belief and doubt. Discovering the hiddenness argument and working it out certainly pushed me further in the direction of outright disbelief or atheism, and eventually that's where I found myself most of the time. But even after that I converted to theism for a short while (or backslid—take your pick), only to be returned to atheism by a double jolt of reasoning: hiddenness reasoning together with the philosophical problem of evil in a particularly acute form.

I've been all over the map in relation to belief in God; I am personally and intimately acquainted with every relevant attitude. The God business can be, and was at times for me, a messy business—not a matter of thinking through some arguments and seeing exactly where to stand forever and ever, amen. Things are more complicated than that. Nonetheless the truth-seeker will persevere and seek to meet philosophy's challenge. And if the truth seems to be that God does not exist, then she will not be afraid to say so. Philosophical inquiry, like all inquiry, seeks results, and although the decision can be hard to make, sometimes one needs just to place a big check mark on one's list and move on. "Truthing" is another new word, which takes "truth" and turns it into a verb. It means telling the truth, particularly a difficult one, about someone or something. The philosopher will prefer truthing to truthiness. And this also when, after considering objections, counter-arguments, and one's religious experiences and gut feelings, the hiddenness argument still looks convincing.

By now I've been a nonbeliever longer than a believer, and I've discovered that that bland designation—"nonbeliever"—in fact obscures a whole host of new possibilities that allow one to transcend entirely the triumvirate of theism, atheism, and agnosticism. For me, there have not been any new possibilities of non-theistic religious belief, so I remain a nonbeliever even in the larger sense. But experiences of prolonged and intense intellectual concentration as well as powerful non-theistic religious experiences for which I was freed only by losing belief in God, have helped to teach me that opening myself to life and wonder—synonymous when all's well—is the only way to go.

CODA

After Personal Gods

Some who accept the final conclusion of the hiddenness argument will respond to our discussion by saying "Just as I thought!" Others will find that result much more disconcerting or even depressing. To both I say that this is not the end of the story, religiously speaking.

In our culture people who think about whether there is a God and conclude there isn't will commonly infer—whether gladly or sadly but rarely indifferently—that blind nature is all there is. They become (to use the philosophical term for their position) *metaphysical naturalists.* This is largely because of how influential the natural sciences have come to be in our culture. Science has given many people a great and often unthinking optimism that everything there is will turn out to have the character of everything science has studied: namely, that of belonging to a system governed entirely by natural law.

I want to suggest that after arriving at the conclusion that no personal God exists, which is to say at atheism, our next move, intellectually speaking, should *not* be to metaphysical naturalism, which would have us close the door to a serious exploration of religious possibilities, but rather to a sort of *agnosticism.* This will not be agnosticism as we've come to know it in our culture, where it competes with atheism, but a *new* agnosticism. The old agnostic found herself in doubt as to whether there is a God. The new agnostic is ready to disbelieve; she is an atheist. But when telling you this, she will add that the God of theism is just the last of the exclusively personal gods, and who knows what may come next? Ultimism is too impressive an idea for us rightly to suppose it exhausted by personal gods.

Ironically, this position can be provided with a scientific basis—one associated with the concept of deep time briefly introduced in Chapter 6 and more fully discussed in my earlier book for a general audience, *Evolutionary Religion*.

Deep time is more than the deep past, though the past is what we tend to focus on (we focused on it in Chapter 6). Deep time also includes the deep future. With sciences such as geology and astronomy working together, a pretty clear picture has recently emerged of a planet that—to borrow from the last page of Charles Darwin's *Origin of Species*—has "gone cycling on" for billions of years in the past and, left to its own devices, will do so for billions of years more. Remarkably, for at least one billion of those years more, so science tells us, the Earth will remain hospitable to life.

It's both shocking and exhilarating mentally to place the human career as we've known it thus far at the *back* end of that billion years. Turning one's head from past to future, one can see how incredibly short a distance intelligent life on our planet has traveled in scientific time. If the time available is compared to a mile, our few thousand years of serious inquiry have moved us forward less than half an inch! Of course we may not get much further. But the possibilities alone, for ourselves or species to come, are breathtaking. If science should—and of course it should—thrill us with its discovery of the place of Earth in the solar system, the place of the solar system in the universe, and the place of humans in the broad tapestry of life, it should thrill us too with its discovery of *our place in time*. But this discovery we haven't yet absorbed. Not many heads have turned.

When the future turn does take place—or, better, when we have learned to look both ways, to the deep future as well as to the deep past—we'll notice the need for some evolution in our thinking. And some of this needed evolution concerns religion.

Two things in particular we'll see. First, that we have even more reason to wonder whether religious beliefs from the past involving gods much like us are intellectually fit to survive. Can we really trust the thoughts on ultimate things of a species as immature as ours? Second, that we may have only dipped our toes, so far, in an ocean of religious possibilities. Some of those possibilities may even be realized. Our primitivity and the poverty of our imagination *may* be such that the profoundest visions of mystics and seers give only the slightest taste of what reality actually has to offer in the way of religious truths science can't reach.

Of course, and by the same token, it may be that science will in time tell us everything there is to know about the broad structure of reality. Metaphysical naturalism may turn out to be true. Who can deny it? But who aware of our place in time will affirm that it has *already* turned out to be true, after having disproved the existence of only the last of the person-like gods? Those who insist on doing so—and, as I've noted, they are legion—are on shaky ground. They should have looked both ways before crossing the road to this unstable position.

So to what more stable position might they retreat—or ascend? Where should all of us find ourselves after concluding that the God of theism does not exist? Enter the new agnosticism.

The old agnosticism, as I've already mentioned, meant neither believing nor disbelieving in the existence of a person-like God. The new agnostics go beyond this. On the basis of such reasoning as that of the hiddenness argument, they believe there is no person-like God. This conclusion, they say, our familiarity with persons can already deliver for us. But they neither believe nor disbelieve the more general claim of ultimism, which amounts to the claim *that there is some reality worth calling religious.* Their agnosticism pushes us forward from what you might call a lower-order focus on the idea of God to a higher-order focus on the idea that God is said to realize, but which can be filled out in many different ways we have only begun to explore: the idea of something at once deepest in the nature of things and possessed of the greatest possible inherent value and significance. (Perhaps such a reality would even in some way include personal elements—it need not be *im*personal—though, if theism is false, it could not be defined by them.) Here we see why the new agnosticism can subsume atheism. For even if you deny that ultimism is realized in this *one* way described by theism, you may experience no more than doubt when you consider whether it is realized in *some* way.

What is the upshot? Just this. That neither complacency nor despair should be our attitude upon concluding with the hiddenness argument that the traditional God of theism does not exist. Having concluded that no such God exists, the safest and also most intellectually adventurous next move is not to metaphysical naturalism—as though the idea of personal gods is the best our species can do!—but rather, with our vision enlarged by thoughts of deep time, onward to the next level of investigation into ultimate things. If we accept this positive challenge, and if, in time, the brighter possibilities here are realized, then the hiddenness of the *traditional* God will only have had the effect of allowing the *real* God—ultimate reality as it truly is—to be more clearly revealed.

NOTES

Preface

vii **Some variety has already emerged.** See, in particular, Theodore Drange (1998) *Nonbelief & Evil: Two Arguments for the Nonexistence of God*, Amherst, MA: Prometheus Press, and Stephen Maitzen (2006) "Divine Hiddenness and the Demographics of Theism," *Religious Studies* 42: 177–91.

viii **I put together such an argument in my first book.** See J. L. Schellenberg (1993) *Divine Hiddenness and Human Reason*, Ithaca, NY: Cornell University Press.

x **my previous book.** See J. L. Schellenberg (2013) *Evolutionary Religion*, Oxford: Oxford University Press.

Chapter 1

1 **a clear framework for understanding everything else I say about logic and related matters.** Readers who would like some more help may consult one of the many available introductory texts, such as Wilfred Hodges (2001) *Logic: An Introduction to Elementary Logic* 2nd edn, London: Penguin Books.

Chapter 2

14 **Theologians have long spoken of the hiddenness of God.** For a fairly recent example which illustrates how widely the notion came to be applied in the twentieth century, see Karl Barth (1957) *Church Dogmatics*, vol. 2, pt. 1, Edinburgh: T&T Clark, p. 187. Barth writes: "That God is, lies as little in the field of our spiritual oversight and control as what He is. We lack the capacity both to establish His existence and to define His being." One of his chapter sub-headings is "The Hiddenness of God."

18 **In 2003 I chose the word "ultimism" to fill the empty space.** This was while working on a book that came out two years later: J. L. Schellenberg (2005) *Prolegomena to a Philosophy of Religion*, Ithaca, NY: Cornell University Press. Ultimism, as I understand it, was first introduced and discussed in chapter 1 of that work.

20 **In the second chapter of his *Proslogion*, he spun the famous ontological argument.** See Proslogion 2 in Brian Davies and G. R. Evans (Eds.) (1998) *Anselm of Canterbury: The Major Works*, Oxford: Oxford University Press.

Chapter 3

23 **my critics in philosophy have done the same.** An especially clear example is provided by the University of Delaware philosopher Jeffrey J. Jordan, by no means an atheist, who said this in the context of an internet debate: "John Schellenberg has presented an argument noteworthy in several respects. One interesting respect is that his 'divine hiddenness' argument is a philosophically interesting innovation in a debate that has raged for millennia. Innovation in philosophy, especially an interesting innovation, is not an easy task, but Professor Schellenberg has accomplished it." "The Sounds of Silence: Why the Divine Hiddenness Argument Fails": <http://www.infidels.org/library/modern/jeffrey_jordan/silence.html> accessed July 11, 2014.

24 **put a lot of thoughts about the hiddenness of God (literally construed) into his *Pensées*.** The translation I have studied is that by A. J. Krailsheimer (1966) Harmondsworth: Penguin. My references are to its pages and to Krailsheimer's numbering of the fragments.

24 **"'If I had seen a miracle,' they say, 'I should be converted'."** *Pensées* fragment 378, p. 137.

25 **"If this religion boasted..."** *Pensées* fragment 427, p. 155.

25 **"If the evidence of revelation appears doubtful, this itself turns into a positive argument against it..."** Joseph Butler, *The Analogy of Religion, Natural and Revealed, to the Constitution and Course of Nature*, in J. H. Bernard (Ed.) (1900) *The Works of Bishop Butler*, London: Macmillan, vol. 2, pt. 2, chap. 6, par. 1.

26 **"A god who is all-knowing and all-powerful and who does not even make sure his creatures understand his intentions..."** Friedrich Nietzsche, *Daybreak*, R. J. Holingdale [Trans.] (1982) New York: Cambridge University Press, pp. 89–90.

27 **There are various versions of the story.** One appears in John R. Searle (1998) *Mind, Language, and Society: Philosophy in the Real World*, New York: Basic Books, p. 36.

27 **"There is no single natural happening, nor any constellation of such happenings, which establishes God's existence..."** N. R. Hanson (1971) *What I Do Not Believe and Other Essays*, Dordrecht: Reidel, p. 322.

27 **"One might be tempted to see in... [ambivalent evidence] a vindication of atheism..."** Ronald Hepburn, "From World to God" in Basil Mitchell (Ed.) *Philosophy of Religion*, Oxford: Oxford University Press, p. 178.

28 **According to Schlesinger, a perfectly *just* God.** See George Schlesinger, "The Availability of Evidence in Support of Religious Belief" (1984), *Faith and Philosophy* 1: 422–7. See also George Schlesinger (1988) *New Perspectives on Old-Time Religion*, Oxford: Oxford University Press, pp. 172ff.

28 **Hepburn was joined by John Hick and my own teacher, Terence Penelhum.** See, for example, John Hick (1966) *Faith and Knowledge*, 2nd edn, Ithaca, NY: Cornell University Press, p. 187, and Terence Penelhum (1971), *Religion and Rationality*, New York: Random House, p. 206.

29 **Thus the hiddenness argument, so it may be said, still reduces to an argument from evil.** For an example of this view, see C. Stephen Evans (2010) *Natural Signs and Knowledge of God: A New Look at Theistic Arguments*, Oxford: Oxford University Press, pp. 164–5.

30 **It follows that the hiddenness argument and the problem of evil are distinct.** For a fuller development of this view, see J. L. Schellenberg (2010) "The Hiddenness Problem and the Problem of Evil," *Faith and Philosophy* 27: 45–60.

32 **finely detailed by Charles Taylor in his doorstop of a book *A Secular Age*.** See Charles Taylor (2007) *A Secular Age*, Cambridge, MA: Harvard University Press.

33 **remarked upon by Steven Pinker in his own doorstop *The Better Angels of our Nature*.** See Steven Pinker (2011) *The Better Angels of our Nature: Why Violence Has Declined*, New York: Viking, pp. 571–92.

Chapter 4

36 **you could see that each side—in fact *multiple* sides—had persuasive ways of making sense of human experience in their own terms.** And my favorite teacher at the time kept writing about the importance of religious ambiguity—for example, in Terence Penelhum (1983) *God and Skepticism*, Dordrecht: Reidel, pp. 156–8.

43 **I don't know how many times I've had to correct, in print, the idea that I think a loving God would be open to relationship with us mainly or only because such a relationship would contribute to our well-being.** Here are some examples of me correcting the error: J. L. Schellenberg (2005) "The Hiddenness Argument Revisited (I)," *Religious Studies* 41: 207, 210 (cf. 202). And here is an example of the error still being made: C. Stephen Evans (2010) *Natural Signs and Knowledge of God: A New Look at Theistic Arguments*, Oxford: Oxford University Press, p. 163.

43 **divine love at *some* time must involve openness to a sharing relationship.** That everyone will accept this is suggested by the discussion of love in Eleonore Stump (2012) *Wandering in Darkness: Narrative and the Problem of Suffering*, Oxford: Oxford University Press—and here I have in mind both the fact that Stump, a fairly conservative Catholic philosopher, insists that a desire for union with the beloved is necessarily part of love, and also the many careful arguments by which she defends this view and turns aside alternatives.

44 **But isn't this kind and even loving of Fred, rather than un-loving?** I owe this example to Alexander Pruss. See the blog discussion here: <http://prosblogion.ektopos.com/2014/10/06/hiddenness-and-the-necessary-condition-fallacy/>. Accessed January 16, 2015.

Chapter 5

54 **And such free will, most theists and also many non-theists will say.** Interesting arguments defending the importance of free will in contexts like this can be found in Bruce Langtry (2008) *God, the Best, and Evil*, Oxford: Oxford University Press. Much of this work will be tough going for the uninitiated, but Langtry's reasoning about free will is frequently accessible.

58 **Perhaps someone will still be inclined to resist by saying that *hope* or even a certain kind of beliefless *faith* could replace belief.** I thank Dan Howard-Snyder for pressing me on this point. Related arguments appear in several papers, including Andrew Cullison (2010) "Two Solutions to the Problem of Divine Hiddenness," *American Philosophical Quarterly* 47: 119–35.

59 **the relationship made possible by belief is a different relationship.** Suppose you're a philosopher and you disagree with the point I've been making. Here is a comment just for you. Without losing force, the hiddenness argument to follow can be slightly revised to circumvent this issue and allow acceptance of the idea that nonbelieving hope or faith would make an adequate initial basis for loving relationship. Just revise the relevant part of the argument in such a way that, instead of referring to nonresistant nonbelief, it refers to *nonresistantly being in a cognitive condition, in relation to the proposition that God exists, that is incompatible with then being able to participate in a personal relationship with God just by trying*, with this cognitive condition conjunctively construed, cashed out in terms of being nonbelieving *and* without nonbelieving faith *and* without nonbelieving hope. And then also make the appropriate corresponding revisions elsewhere in the argument. I myself think this cognitive condition need not be thus construed, since it clearly is as stated in the text. But even if you disagree, by introducing a conjunctive alternative you will not prevent the hiddenness argument from succeeding, since there are or have been plenty of finite persons, capable of personal relationship with God and nonresistant, who instantiate all of its conjuncts.

61 **Avoidance of a negative response to God that harms the future prospects of the relationship.** For such an approach, see, for example, Daniel Howard-Snyder (1996) "The Argument from Divine Hiddenness," *Canadian Journal of Philosophy* 26: 433–53 and Travis Dumsday (2010) "Divine Hiddenness, Free-Will, and the Victims of Wrongdoing," *Faith and Philosophy* 27: 423–38.

62 **"The God of the Christians is a God of love and consolation..."** Blaise Pascal, *Pensées*, A. J. Krailsheimer (Trans.) (1966) Harmondsworth: Penguin, Fragment 449, p. 169.

64 **Genuine or deep freedom to choose one's own destiny, morally speaking.** For this approach, see, for example, Richard Swinburne (1988) *Providence and the Problem of Evil*, Oxford: Clarendon Press, chap. 11 and Michael J. Murray (2002) "Deus Absconditus" in Daniel Howard-Snyder and Paul Moser (Eds.) *Divine Hiddenness: New Essays*, New York: Cambridge University Press.

68 **A chance to develop deep longing for God, which might help someone grow spiritually and so should be viewed as a good thing.** For this approach see, for example, Trent Dougherty and Ted Poston (2007) "Divine Hiddenness and the Nature of Belief," *Religious Studies* 43: 183–98.

69 **what the Spanish mystic, St. John of the Cross, called "the dark night of the soul."** See "Dark Night of the Soul," II, 11, 3, in Kieran Kavanaugh and Otilio Rodriguez (Trans.) *The Collected Works of St. John of the Cross*, Washington: ICS Publications.

69 **The opportunity to exhibit a noble sort of courage or love that sacrifices itself for the good even where no belief in a happy afterlife exists to diminish its value.** For this approach, see Andrew Cullison (2010) "Two Solutions to the Problem of Divine Hiddenness," *American Philosophical Quarterly* 47: 119–35.

70 **The possibility of cooperative investigation into God's existence.** See Richard Swinburne (1998) *Providence and the Problem of Evil*, Oxford: Clarendon Press, chap. 11.

Chapter 6

75 **Some writers responding to the hiddenness argument have proceeded in just this manner.** See, for example, Douglas Henry (2001) "Does Reasonable Nonbelief Exist?" *Faith and Philosophy* 18: 75–92 and Robert T. Lehe (2004) "A Response to the Argument from the Reasonableness of Nonbelief," *Faith and Philosophy* 21: 159–74.

78 **There's just too much evidence of God-exclusive thought forms among hunter-gatherers both then and now.** This appears in many places, but see, for example, Pascal Boyer (2001) *Religion Explained: The*

Evolutionary Origins of Religious Thought, New York: Basic Books and Scott Atran (2002) *In Gods We Trust: The Evolutionary Landscape of Religion*, Oxford: Oxford University Press.

78 **But as Robert Wright shows.** The quotations that follow are taken from Robert Wright (2009) *The Evolution of God*, New York: Little, Brown and Company, pp. 19, 21.

79 **It has proved tempting for some.** See, for example, Robert T. Lehe (2004) "A Response to the Argument from the Reasonableness of Nonbelief," *Faith and Philosophy* 21: 159–74.

81 **But I've heard many similar testimonies.** Some are recorded in Russell Blackford and Udo Schuklenk (Eds.) *50 Voices of Disbelief: Why We Are Atheists*, Oxford: Blackwell.

Chapter 7

89 **I might have made this chapter the first in our series.** In my latest and most formal presentation of the hiddenness argument for academic philosophers (see J. L. Schellenberg (forthcoming) "Divine Hiddenness and Human Philosophy" in Adam Green and Eleonore Stump (Eds.) *Hidden Divinity and Religious Belief: New Perspectives*, Cambridge: Cambridge University Press), I do put the love premise first:

(1) If God exists, then God is perfectly loving toward such finite persons as there may be. [Premise]

(2) If God is perfectly loving toward such finite persons as there may be, then for any capable finite person S and time t, God is at t open to being in a positively meaningful and conscious relationship (a personal relationship) with S at t. [Premise]

(3) If God exists, then for any capable finite person S and time t, God is at t open to being in a personal relationship with S at t. [1, 2 by Hypothetical Syllogism].

(4) If for any capable finite person S and time t, God is at t open to being in a personal relationship with S at t, then for any capable finite person S and time t, it is not the case that S is at t nonresistantly in a state of nonbelief in relation to the proposition that God exists. [Premise]

(5) If God exists, then for any capable finite person S and time t, it is not the case that S is at t nonresistantly in a state of nonbelief in relation to the proposition that God exists. [3, 4 by Hypothetical Syllogism]

(6) There is at least one capable finite person S and time t such that S is or was at t nonresistantly in a state of nonbelief in relation to the proposition that God exists. [Premise]

(7) It is not the case that God exists. [5, 6 by Modus Tollens].

90 **There's a moving story.** See Elie Wiesel (1979) *The Trial of God*, New York: Random House.

91 **The philosopher Xenophanes, for example.** See Norman Melchert (2002), *The Great Conversation, vol. 1: Pre-Socratics through Descartes*, 4th edn, New York: McGraw-Hill, pp. 15–16.

92 **Notice, for example, how both philosophers and theologians have greeted the work of "new atheists" such as Richard Dawkins.** The most recent of many examples is David Bentley Hart (2013) *The Experience of God: Being, Consciousness, Bliss*, New Haven: Yale University Press.

101 **As the philosopher and religious thinker Robert Merrihew Adams has recently done.** See Robert M. Adams (1987) *The Virtue of Faith*, New York: Oxford University Press, pp. 187–8.

Chapter 8

105 **the argument has often been misinterpreted in its short 25-year history.** In a two-part discussion in the journal *Religious Studies* in 2005, the entire first part had to be devoted to explaining and correcting misinterpretations of the argument. See J. L. Schellenberg (2005) "The Hiddenness Argument Revisited (I)," *Religious Studies* 41: 201–15.

111 **Opponents of the hiddenness argument sometimes develop the objection that there might very well be goods *unknown* to us.** See, for example, Michael Bergmann (2009) "Skeptical Theism and the Problem of Evil" in Thomas P. Flint and Michael C. Rea (Eds.) *The Oxford Handbook of Philosophical Theology*, New York: Oxford University Press.

113 **The complex cumulative case put forward by my former supervisor at Oxford, Richard Swinburne.** See Richard Swinburne (2004) *The Existence of God*, 2nd edn, Oxford: Oxford University Press.

114 **Instead, this very different answer appeals to *experiences apparently of God*.** The fountainhead for much of this discussion is William P. Alston (1991) *Perceiving God: The Epistemology of Religious Experience*, Ithaca, NY: Cornell University Press.

116 **"the quality of preferring concepts or facts one wishes to be true, rather than concepts or facts known to be true."** This definition and the Colbert story can be found at <http://www.americandialect.org/2006/01>: accessed August 1, 2014.

RECENT WORK ON DIVINE HIDDENNESS

Aijaz, I. and Weidler, M. (2007) "Some Critical Reflections on the Hiddenness Argument," *International Journal for Philosophy of Religion* 61: 1–23.

Aijaz, I. and Weidler, M. (2013) "Divine Hiddenness and Discrimination: A Philosophical Dilemma," *Sophia* 52: 95–114.

Bergmann, M. (2009) "Skeptical Theism and the Problem of Evil" in T. Flint and M. Rea (Eds.), *Oxford Handbook of Philosophical Theology*, Oxford: Oxford University Press, 374–99.

Bishop, J. (2007) *Believing by Faith: An Essay in the Epistemology and Ethics of Religious Belief*, Oxford: Clarendon Press, chapter 4.

Brown, H. (2013) "Incarnation and the Divine Hiddenness Debate," *Heythrop Journal* 54: 252–60.

Coffman, E. J. and Cervantes, J. (2011) "Hiddenness, Evidence, and Idolatry" in R. van Arragon and K. J. Clark (Eds.), *Evidence and Religious Belief*, Oxford: Oxford University Press, 95–113.

Cordry, B. (2008) "Divine Hiddenness and Belief *De Re*," *Religious Studies* 45: 1–19.

Corrigan, R. (2007) *Why Hidden? Divine Hiddenness, Love, and Revelation*, New York: Parmenion Press.

Cosculluela, V. (1996) "Bolstering the Argument from Non-Belief," *Religious Studies* 32: 507–12.

Cullison, A. (2010) "Two Solutions to the Problem of Divine Hiddenness," *American Philosophical Quarterly* 47: 119–34.

Cuneo, T. (2013) "Another Look at Divine Hiddenness" in D. Howard-Snyder (Ed.), *Special Issue: Critical Essays on J. L. Schellenberg's Philosophy of Religion, Religious Studies* 49: 151–64.

Davis, S. (2001) "A Reply to Paul K. Moser's 'Divine Hiding'," *Philosophia Christi* 3: 109–11.

Davis, S. (2005) "Is Nonbelief a Proof of Atheism?" *Philo* 8: 151–9.

DeWeese, G. (2001) "Toward a Robust Natural Theology: A Reply to Paul K. Moser's 'Divine Hiding'," *Philosophia Christi* 3: 113–17.

Dougherty, T. and Parker, R. (2013) "Divine Hiddenness" in Tim Crane (Ed.), *Routledge Encyclopedia of Philosophy*, London: Routledge.

Drange, T. (1993) "The Argument from Non-Belief," *Religious Studies* 29: 417–32.

Drange, T. (1998a) "Nonbelief vs. Lack of Evidence: Two Atheological Arguments," *Philo* 1: 105–14.

Drange, T. (1998b) *Nonbelief & Evil: Two Arguments for the Nonexistence of God*, Amherst, MA: Prometheus Press.
Drange, T. (2002) "McHugh's Expectations Dashed," *Philo* 5: 242–8.
Drange, T. (2005) "Reply to Critics," *Philo* 8: 169–82.
Draper, P. (2002) "Seeking But Not Believing: Confessions of a Practicing Agnostic" in D. Howard-Snyder and P. K. Moser (Eds.), *Divine Hiddenness: New Essays*, Cambridge: Cambridge University Press, 197–214.
Dumsday, T. (2010a) "Divine Hiddenness and the Responsibility Argument: Assessing Schellenberg's Argument against Theism," *Philosophia Christi* 12: 357–71.
Dumsday, T. (2010b) "Divine Hiddenness, Free Will, and the Victims of Wrongdoing," *Faith and Philosophy* 27: 423–38.
Dumsday, T. (2011) "Divine Hiddenness as Divine Mercy," *Religious Studies* 48: 183–98.
Dumsday, T. (2012) "Divine Hiddenness and Creaturely Resentment," *International Journal for Philosophy of Religion* 72: 41–51.
Dumsday, T. (2013) "A Thomistic Response to the Problem of Hiddenness," *American Catholic Philosophical Quarterly* 87: 365–77.
Dumsday, T. (2014) "Divine Hiddenness and Divine Humility," *Sophia* 53: 51–64.
Dumsday, T. (forthcoming) "Divine Hiddenness and the Opiate of the People," *International Journal for Philosophy of Religion*.
Evans, C. S. (2006) "Can God be Hidden and Evident at the Same Time? Some Kierkegaardian Reflections," *Faith and Philosophy* 23: 241–53.
Evans, C. S. (2010) *Natural Signs and Knowledge of God*, Oxford: Oxford University Press, 159–69.
Ferreira, M. J. (2002) "A Kierkegaardian View of Divine Hiddenness" in D. Howard-Snyder and P. K. Moser (Eds.), *Divine Hiddenness: New Essays*, Cambridge: Cambridge University Press, 164–80.
Garcia, L. (2002) "St. John of the Cross and the Necessity of Divine Hiddenness" in D. Howard-Snyder and P. K. Moser (Eds.), *Divine Hiddenness: New Essays*, Cambridge: Cambridge University Press, 83–97.
Henry, D. (2001) "Does Reasonable Nonbelief Exist?" *Faith and Philosophy* 18: 75–92.
Henry, D. (2008) "Reasonable Doubts about Reasonable Nonbelief," *Faith and Philosophy* 25: 276–89.
Hick, J. (1989) *An Interpretation of Religion: Human Responses to the Transcendent*, London: Macmillan, Part II.
Howard-Snyder, D. (1996) "The Argument from Divine Hiddenness," *Canadian Journal of Philosophy* 26: 433–53.
Howard-Snyder, D. (2005) "Hiddenness of God" in D. Borchert (Ed.), *Encyclopedia of Philosophy* [2nd Edn], Vol. 4., London: MacMillan, 352–7.
Howard-Snyder, D. (forthcoming) "Divine Hiddenness," *Stanford Encyclopedia of Philosophy*.

Howard-Snyder, D. and Moser, P. K. (2002) "Introduction: the Hiddenness of God" in D. Howard-Snyder and P. K. Moser (Eds.), *Divine Hiddenness: New Essays*, Cambridge: Cambridge University Press, 1–23.

Janzen, G. (2010) "Is God's Belief Requirement Rational?" *Religious Studies* 47: 465–78.

Jordan, J. (2006) *Pascal's Wager: Pragmatic Arguments and Belief in God*, Oxford: Clarendon Press, chapter 7.

Jordan, J. (2012) "The Topography of Divine Love," *Faith and Philosophy* 29: 53–69.

Jordan, J. (2008) "The Sounds of Silence: Why the Divine Hiddenness Argument Fails" in *God or Blind Nature? Philosophers Debate the Evidence*, at <http://www.infidels.org/library/modern/jeffrey_jordan/silence.html>.

Keller, J. (1995) "The Hiddenness of God and the Problem of Evil," *International Journal for Philosophy of Religion* 37: 13–24.

Keller, J. (2007) "Another Problem of Evil: Divine Hiddenness," chapter 3 of *Problems of Evil and the Power of God*, Aldershot: Ashgate.

King, R. (2008) *Obstacles to Divine Revelation: God and the Reorientation of Human Reason*, London: Continuum, chapter 9.

Kinghorn, P. (2005) *The Decision of Faith: Can Christian Beliefs be Freely Chosen?* London: T&T Clark, chapter 7.

Kvanvig, J. (2002) "Divine Hiddenness: What is the Problem?" in D. Howard-Snyder and P. K. Moser (Eds.), *Divine Hiddenness: New Essays*, Cambridge: Cambridge University Press, 149–63.

Lehe, R. (2004) "A Response to the Argument from the Reasonableness of Nonbelief," *Faith and Philosophy* 21: 159–74.

Lovering, R. (2004) "Divine Hiddenness and Inculpable Ignorance," *International Journal for Philosophy of Religion* 56: 89–107.

Lovering, R. (2013) *God and Evidence: Problems for Theistic Philosophers*, New York: Bloomsbury, chapter 3.

McBrayer, J. (2006) "On 'A Molinist-Style Response to Schellenberg', by Michael Thune," *Southwest Philosophy Review* 22: 71–7.

McBrayer, J. and Swenson, P. (2011) "Scepticism about the Argument from Divine Hiddenness," *Religious Studies* 48: 129–50.

McCreary, M. (2010) "Schellenberg on Divine Hiddenness and Religious Scepticism," *Religious Studies* 46: 207–25.

McHugh, C. (2002) "A Refutation of Drange's Arguments from Evil and Nonbelief," *Philo* 5: 94–100.

McKim, R. (1990) "The Hiddenness of God," *Religious Studies* 26: 141–61.

McKim, R. (2001) *Religious Ambiguity and Religious Diversity*, Oxford: Oxford University Press.

Maitzen, S. (2006) "Divine Hiddenness and the Demographics of Theism," *Religious Studies* 42: 177–91.

Maitzen, S. (2008) "Does Molinism Explain the Demographics of Theism?" *Religious Studies* 44: 473–7.

Marsh, J. (2008) "Do the Demographics of Theistic Belief Disconfirm Theism? A Reply to Maitzen," *Religious Studies* 44: 465–71.

Marsh, J. (2013) "Darwin and the Problem of Natural Nonbelief," *The Monist* 96: 349–76.

Mawson, T. (2012) "The Rationality of Classical Theism and its Demographics" in Y. Nagasawa (Ed.), *Scientific Approaches to the Philosophy of Religion*, London: Palgrave Macmillan, 184–202.

Morris, T. (1988) "The Hidden God," *Philosophical Topics* 16: 5–21.

Moser, P. K. (2001a) "Divine Hiding," *Philosophia Christi* 3: 91–107.

Moser, P. K. (2001b) "A God Who Hides and Seeks: A Response to Davis and DeWeese," *Philosophia Christi* 3: 119–25.

Moser, P. K. (2002) "Cognitive Idolatry and Divine Hiding" in D. Howard-Snyder and P. K. Moser (Eds.), *Divine Hiddenness: New Essays*, Cambridge: Cambridge University Press, 120–48.

Moser, P. K. (2004a) "Divine Hiddenness does not Justify Atheism" in M. Peterson and R. vanArragon (Eds.), *Contemporary Debates* in *Philosophy of Religion*, Malden, MA: Blackwell, 42–53.

Moser, P. K. (2004b) "Reply to Schellenberg" in M. Peterson and R. vanArragon (Eds.), *Contemporary Debates* in *Philosophy of Religion*, Malden, MA: Blackwell, 56–8.

Moser, P. K. (2008a) "Divine Hiddenness, Death, and Meaning" in P. Copan and C. Meister (Eds.), *Philosophy of Religion: Classic and Contemporary Issues*, Oxford: Blackwell, 215–27. [Reprinted in *The Philosophy of Religion Reader*, ed. C. Meister (London: Routledge, 2008), 613–24.]

Moser, P. K. (2008b) *The Elusive God: Reorienting Religious Epistemology*, Cambridge: Cambridge University Press.

Murray, M. (1993) "Coercion and the Hiddenness of God," *American Philosophical Quarterly* 30: 27–38.

Murray, M. (2002) "Deus Absconditus" in D. Howard-Snyder and P. K. Moser (Eds.), *Divine Hiddenness: New Essays*, Cambridge: Cambridge University Press, 62–82.

Murray, M. and Rea, M. (2009) *An Introduction to the Philosophy of Religion*, Cambridge: Cambridge University Press, 180–9.

Murray, M. and Taylor, D. E. (2007) "Hiddenness" in C. Meister and P. Copan (Eds.), *The Routledge Companion to Philosophy of Religion*, New York: Routledge, 308–17.

Napier, S. (2008) *Virtue Epistemology: Motivation and Knowledge*, London: Continuum, chapter 7.

Oakes, R. (2008) "Life, Death, and the Hiddenness of God," *International Journal for Philosophy of Religion* 64: 155–60.

O'Connell, J. H. (2013) "Divine Hiddenness: Would More Miracles Solve the Problem?" *Heythrop Journal* 54: 261–7.

Penelhum, T. (1983) *God and Skepticism: A Study in Skepticism and Fideism*, Dordrecht: Reidel, chapters 5 and 7.

Penelhum, T. (1995) *Reason and Religious Faith*, Boulder, CO: Westview Press, chapter 6.

Philipse, H. (2012) *God in the Age of Science? A Critique of Religious Reason*, Oxford: Oxford University Press, 302–9.

Poston, T. and Dougherty, T. (2007) "Divine Hiddenness and the Nature of Belief," *Religious Studies* 43: 183–98.

Rea, M. (2009) "Narrative, Liturgy, and the Hiddenness of God" in K. Timpe (Ed.), *Metaphysics and God: Essays in Honour of Eleonore Stump*, New York: Routledge, 76–96.

Rea, M. (2011) "Divine Hiddenness, Divine Silence" in L. Pojman and M. Rea (Eds.), *Philosophy of Religion: An Anthology*, 6th ed., Boston: Wadsworth/Cengage, 266–75.

Roark, E. (2005) "The Necessarily Moral Aspect of Divine Hiddenness," *Southwest Philosophical Studies* 27: 76–81.

Ross, J. J. (2002) "The Hiddenness of God: A Puzzle or a Real Problem" in D. Howard-Snyder and P. K. Moser (Eds.), *Divine Hiddenness: New Essays*, Cambridge: Cambridge University Press, 181–96.

Rowe, W. (1996) "The Evidential Argument from Evil: A Second Look" in D. Howard-Snyder (Ed.), *The Evidential Argument from Evil*, Bloomington: Indiana University Press, 262–85.

Rowe, W. (2001) "Skeptical Theism: A Response to Bergmann," *Noûs* 35: 297–303.

Schellenberg, J. L. (1993) *Divine Hiddenness and Human Reason*, Ithaca, NY: Cornell University Press.

Schellenberg, J. L. (1996) "Response to Howard-Snyder," *Canadian Journal of Philosophy* 26: 455–62.

Schellenberg, J. L. (2002) "What the Hiddenness of God Reveals: A Collaborative Discussion" in D. Howard-Snyder and P. K. Moser (Eds.), *Divine Hiddenness: New Essays*, Cambridge: Cambridge University Press.

Schellenberg, J. L. (2004a) "Divine Hiddenness Justifies Atheism," in M. Peterson and R. vanArragon (Eds.), *Contemporary Debates in Philosophy of Religion*, Malden, MA: Blackwell, 30–41.

Schellenberg, J. L. (2004b) "Hiddenness Concealed: Reply to Moser," in M. Peterson and R. van Arragon (Eds.), *Contemporary Debates in Philosophy of Religion*, Malden, MA: Blackwell, 54–5.

Schellenberg, J. L. (2005a) "The Hiddenness Argument Revisited (I)," *Religious Studies* 41: 201–15.

Schellenberg, J. L. (2005b) "The Hiddenness Argument Revisited (II)," *Religious Studies* 41: 287–303.

Schellenberg, J. L. (2005c) "On Reasonable Nonbelief and Perfect Love: Replies to Henry and Lehe," *Faith and Philosophy* 22: 330–42.

Schellenberg, J. L. (2006) "Preface" to the paperback edition of *Divine Hiddenness and Human Reason*, Ithaca, NY: Cornell University Press.

Schellenberg, J. L. (2007a) *The Wisdom to Doubt: A Justification of Religious Skepticism*, Ithaca, NY: Cornell University Press, chapters 9 and 10.

Schellenberg, J. L. (2007b) "On not Unnecessarily Darkening the Glass: A Reply to Poston and Dougherty," *Religious Studies* 43: 199–204.

Schellenberg, J. L. (2008a) "What Divine Hiddenness Reveals, or How Weak Theistic Evidence is Strong Atheistic Proof" in *God or Blind Nature? Philosophers Debate the Evidence*, at <http://www.infidels.org/library/modern/john_schellenberg/hidden.html>.

Schellenberg, J. L. (2008b) "The Sounds of Silence Stilled: A Reply to Jordan on Hiddenness" in *God or Blind Nature? Philosophers Debate the Evidence*, at <http://www.infidels.org/library/modern/john_schellenberg/silence-stilled.html>.

Schellenberg, J. L. (2008c) "Reply to Aijaz and Weidler on Hiddenness," *International Journal for Philosophy of Religion* 64: 135–40.

Schellenberg, J. L. (2008d) "Response to Tucker on Hiddenness," *Religious Studies* 44: 289–93.

Schellenberg, J. L. (2010a) "Divine Hiddenness" in C. Taliaferro, P. Draper, and P. Quinn (Eds.), *A Companion to Philosophy of Religion* [2nd Edn], Malden, MA: Wiley-Blackwell, 509–18.

Schellenberg, J. L. (2010b) "How to be an Atheist and a Sceptic Too: Response to McCreary," *Religious Studies* 46: 227–32.

Schellenberg, J. L. (2010c) "The Hiddenness Problem and the Problem of Evil," *Faith and Philosophy* 27: 45–60.

Schellenberg, J. L. (2011) "Would a Loving God Hide from Anyone? Assembling and Assessing the Hiddenness Argument for Atheism" in D. McDermid (Ed.), *Introducing Philosophy for Canadians: A Text With Integrated Readings*, Oxford: Oxford University Press.

Schellenberg, J. L. (forthcoming) "Divine Hiddenness and Human Philosophy" in A. Green and E. Stump (Eds.), *Hidden Divinity and Religious Belief: New Perspectives*, Cambridge: Cambridge University Press.

Schlesinger, G. (1984) "The Availability of Evidence in Support of Religious Belief," *Faith and Philosophy* 1: 421–36.

Soerensen, J. L. (2013) "The Local Problem of God's Hiddenness: A Critique of van Inwagen's Criterion of Philosophical Success," *International Journal for Philosophy of Religion* 74: 297–314.

Swinburne, R. (1987) "Knowledge from Experience and the Problem of Evil" in W. J. Abraham and S. W. Holtzer (Eds.), *The Rationality of Religious Belief: Essays in Honour of Basil Mitchell*, Oxford: Clarendon Press.

Swinburne, R. (1998) *Providence and the Problem of Evil*, Oxford: Oxford University Press, chapter 11.

Swinburne, R. (2004) "The Argument from Hiddenness" in *The Existence of God* [2nd edn], Oxford: Clarendon Press, 267–72.

Talbot, M. (1989) "Is it Natural to Believe in God?" *Faith and Philosophy* 6: 155–71.

Thune, M. (2006) "A Molinist-Style Response to Schellenberg," *Southwest Philosophy Review* 22: 33–41.

Trakakis, N. (2007a) "The Problem of Divine Hiddenness," chapter 8 of *The God Beyond Belief: In Defence of William Rowe's Evidential Argument from Evil*, Dordrecht: Springer, 189–224.

Trakakis, N. (2007b) "An Epistemically Distant God? A Critique of John Hick's Response to the Problem of Divine Hiddenness," *Heythrop Journal* 48: 214–26.

Trisel, B. A. (2012) "God's Silence as an Epistemological Concern," *Philosophical Forum* 43: 383–93.

Tucker, C. (2008) "Divine Hiddenness and the Value of Divine–Creature Relationships," *Religious Studies* 44: 269–87.

van Inwagen, P. (2002) "What Is the Problem of the Hiddenness of God?" in D. Howard-Snyder and P. K. Moser (Eds.), *Divine Hiddenness: New Essays*, Cambridge: Cambridge University Press, 24–32.

van Inwagen, P. (2006) "The Hiddenness of God," Lecture 8 of *The Problem of Evil*, Oxford: Oxford University Press, 135–52.

Wainwright, W. (2002) "Jonathan Edwards and the Hiddenness of God" in D. Howard-Snyder and P. K. Moser (Eds.), *Divine Hiddenness: New Essays*, Cambridge: Cambridge University Press, 98–119.

Wolterstorff, N. (2002) "The Silence of the God Who Speaks" in D. Howard-Snyder and P. K. Moser (Eds.), *Divine Hiddenness: New Essays*, Cambridge: Cambridge University Press, 215–28.

INDEX

Printed and bound by CPI Group (UK) Ltd, Croydon, CR0 4YY